A Mennonite Boy's Odyssey

A Mennonite Boy's Odyssey

Bernard Bowman

Foreword by Gerald W. Gibson

RESOURCE *Publications* · Eugene, Oregon

A MENNONITE BOY'S ODYSSEY

Resource Publications
An Imprint of Wipf and Stock Publishers
199 W. 8th Ave., Suite 3
Eugene, OR 97401

www.wipfandstock.com

PAPERBACK ISBN: 978-1-5326-0271-9
HARDCOVER ISBN: 978-1-5326-0273-3
EBOOK ISBN: 978-1-5326-0272-6

Manufactured in the U.S.A.   SEPTEMBER 19, 2016

Contents

Foreword

BERNIE BOWMAN IS A thinker. Anyone who reads his story in *A Mennonite Boy's Odyssey* can have no doubt of that fact. The account of his odyssey reveals the breadth and depth of his thinking.

Bernie is also a Thinker. The capitalization in this instance reflects his membership in a local discussion group with the name The Thinkers. This group of a dozen members was founded in the early 1950s, when Bernie Bowman was a child, but given its nature and his, it could have been created in anticipation of his joining in 2002. When Bernie began taking his turn as presenter, he quickly became a mainstay of the organization. The topics he selected were well-researched and far-ranging, with titles as diverse as "Gilgamesh—A Man for Our Times," "The Alimentary Canal: An Eclectic Inside Perspective," and "Strings and Other Things—So What?" The titles were always intriguing and the facts and ideas they included so stimulating that we could always count on robust discussion. No wonder The Thinkers came to look with excited anticipation toward Bernie's next paper.

I came to know Bernie long after he was a child, and my knowledge of the Mennonite faith was minimal until I read his story. From the title alone, it is clear that his odyssey had its origins in the Mennonite milieu of his youth. He speaks of his journey as a *spiritual* odyssey, and he elaborates on that fact with honesty in his book. It isn't easy to write about things spiritual in the secular twenty-first century world, but Bernie has taken on the challenge of writing about matters of faith with courage and candor.

Although his odyssey has carried him far from the strictures of the religion of his boyhood, he treats the Mennonite faith and its traditions with respect throughout.

Bernie's Mennonite upbringing was not so different from my own upbringing in a fundamentalist Christian home in the South. As I read *A Mennonite Boy's Odyssey*, that fact struck me and was followed quickly by the question: Why did our odysseys take us to such different destinations? My spiritual journey, like his, had its twists and turns, but our epiphanies were not the same. Other readers, whatever their starting points, will surely find in these pages echoes of their own quests for truth and struggles to reconcile faith and reason. Bernie Bowman's sincere, well-written account of his own odyssey should prove valuable to all who read it in the spirit of its writing.

Dr. Gerald W. Gibson
President Emeritus
Maryville College
Maryville, Tennessee

Acknowledgments

The phrase "No man is an island" is never more true than in the production of a book. This book is no exception. Jim Sturgeon gets special credit for his quiet persistence over the years in telling me my story should be shared. He also read the first pages, offering encouragement to keep writing. Linda Weaver provided many invaluable editing suggestions and assistance with formatting. John Hershberger, PhD, Gerald Gibson, PhD, William Meyer, PhD, and Rufus King all read the manuscript and offered constructive feedback. Gerald also provided the Foreword. Carol, my wife, has been a steady anchor for me to what really matters in life, through all these many years. And, of course, the folks at Wipf and Stock Publishers, in the end, made it possible.

1

A Beginning

An epiphany is a magnificent thing! That moment, suddenly, when it hits you that words—your own or someone else's—perfectly describe what you've known as truth, intuitively. It is that instant when your head and your heart bond in shared understanding. One such epiphany gripped me when reading Scott Peck's book *The Road Less Traveled*.

> Life is difficult. This is a great truth, one of the greatest truths. It is a great truth because once we truly see this truth, we transcend it, once we truly know that life is difficult—once we truly understand and accept it—than [*sic*] life is no longer difficult, because once it is accepted, the fact that life is difficult no longer matters.

Struggle is what forms us; it makes us whole. The "easy button" may bring a smile to our face, it may promise respite from the struggle, but if we think genuinely about it, an easy button for all of life would be a catastrophe.

This book shares my journey of understanding about life over time, my spiritual odyssey over this three score and almost ten years. I do not dwell on personal struggles, not because they were absent, nor because they were inconsequential, but because as I came to understand and accept their countless worth and inescapability, they no longer "mattered," in keeping with Peck's insight.

I do not pretend that my journey is unique or in any way more extraordinary than that of others. It is with that juxtaposition of great humility and great pride that I participate in everyman's journey of conscious development, of asking questions in life. As Leonard Mlodinow so eloquently reminds us in his book entitled *The Upright Thinkers*, our evolving to homo sapiens sapiens from homo sapiens about 40,000 BC brought with it our inquisitiveness, our seeking of answers, our asking, "Why?" And that, to pirate from Robert Frost's poem, has made all the difference.

As you will see in the coming pages, I have made a life by "begging, borrowing, and stealing" from any number of sources. From that gallimaufry of others, both ancient and contemporary, common threads have come together into a coherent life. Someone has said that the source of all genius is to forget one's sources. I lay no claim to being a genius, so I have tried to give credit to my sources throughout. Any omissions are inadvertent and unintended. My story has been a gradual evolvement over time, mostly; however, there have been high points such as the epiphany highlighted above and the Damascus Road experience which follows in the next section. If this, my story, offers any value to you, consider it a gift.

This book is not a criticism of my father. I hope you don't read it that way. My father parented with the best of intentions. He felt it was his God-given obligation to "raise up his children in the way of the Lord." It was just that his "way of the Lord," so untiringly avowed as the "only way," became progressively unworkable for me. I had to find a way of my own, and in so doing I countered, at times, "his way." That is reflected in this odyssey. I carry, to this day, with pride and great appreciation, much of what I heard and saw from my father as relates to one's personal dealings with others. I have tried to reflect that as well in my telling.

Several years after having left my parents' home, I was "back home" at tax season. One of my uncles did accounting and tax returns as part of his business, so I stopped by my uncle's office to catch up and to have him prepare my taxes. I could tell he recognized me, but he just stared at me, saying not a word in response to my rambling greeting. Perhaps it was my long hair, maybe my changing accent from living elsewhere, and no doubt what he considered my hippie attire. I stopped talking and waited; then he said, "Whatever happened to you, boy!" in that slow, Shenandoah Valley draw. Looking back, what had happened was that I had begun my odyssey, my journey, to something other than what he had known of me as a boy.

2

A Damascus Road Experience

It was a Damascus Road encounter. Fall was in full regalia, trees ablaze, with the sun setting in the west behind me as I drove along a two-lane paved road sandwiched between ready-to-harvest corn fields in northeast Iowa. It had been almost two decades since I had taken leave, in my conscious awareness, of the stark heaven or hell dichotomy of the religion of my childhood and adolescence. But somewhere, deep within me, the haunting pull of that religious viewpoint must have retained a lingering hold on me. Was life to be lived pursuing that "carrot" of heaven or dodging that "stick" of hell—or some balance of both? Or could life be worth living for its own sake in the here and now? I thought I had answered that question, but now it came back to me as a crisis of decision. I felt like I was high on a precipice. For someone with acrophobia, it was not a pleasant place to be. I looked back, but I could not turn and go back to that old way of living. Looking ahead lay a vast open vista, clear blue skies and dark mountains and green fields and flowing rivers—but nothing directly ahead to step on. The only way forward was a gigantic leap, off the cliff and into the unknown. Could I plunge forward trusting I had found another way to live and think about life; another way to understand its meaning and purpose? I could not endure on the cliff. The struggle reached its pinnacle. Then in my mind, I leaped!

I felt as if I had instantaneously sprouted wings and began to soar. I rose as if on eagles' wings. I have never landed. That was my Damascus Road experience. This book is my story of life—both before and after.

What was the religion I finally left behind that fateful day? It was the Mennonite faith as expounded by the Virginia Mennonite Conference in the Shenandoah Valley of Virginia in the nineteen-fifties and nineteen-sixties, with a smattering of Appalachian mountain religion. It was the religion of my father. What follows is an introduction to my Father, followed by experiences growing up in the Mennonite Valley culture.

3

Me and My Father

MY FATHER WAS A good man. Folks who dealt with him as a neighbor, relative, friend, or business associate would all agree with that assessment. I knew then, as I know today, he was a good man. But that didn't keep me from feeling estranged from much of his religious and world view. I said estranged from his religious views. I honor, yet today, many of his personal values. Unlike some of my siblings who challenged Dad directly when feeling the unwelcome imposition of his views, I went about my life in his house creating as few waves as possible. I bade my time. I remember saying to a brother in eighth grade, "I just let those words I disagree with roll off my back like water off a duck's back."

You see, it was not easy for my Dad to accept that any of his nine children, four boys and five girls, with me right in the middle at number five, might have a religious viewpoint that differed from his, or that they might approach the world with different values. No doubt he came to his understandings with prodigious thought and conviction; perhaps understandably he felt it was his God-given obligation to instill his way in his children—because he was certain it was God's way. But I came to see it otherwise.

This book is a story about a Mennonite boy who found the religion of his childhood and youth to be inadequate in providing satisfactory answers to the great questions of life. Initially, I focused on questions such as: Where did we come from? Why are we here? Where are we going? Then to questions of meaning—what is our purpose while here? Later the question transitioned more to, "How does one consistently experience being truly alive?"

This Mennonite boy, initially because of discomfort but without intent, then later with purpose, set out on an odyssey seeking a world and religious view that could be both satiating to the soul and intellectually honest for the mind. Along the way I asked myself a simple question, one that I also asked of others, "Does my (or your) particular religious expression or practice tend to make adherents more whole, more fulfilled as human beings?" Worthy religion makes us more whole; it does not harm or quash the person. For me, reconsideration was in order.

If the religion or spiritual ethos that makes you whole is the one you grew up with, then embrace it, run with it. Just be forewarned, this book is the story of someone who felt he had to reconfigure the religion he saw modeled as a child.

You may ask, what about your mother? She was a deeply religious person, always very supportive of my Dad. But she was not the one who set the religious tenor or expectations in the household. What was this faith my mother modeled and my father explicated so unswervingly for my siblings and me?

4

Mennonite Experience in the Shenandoah Valley in the Nineteen-Fifties and Sixties

One's Appearance/Attire

MY FAMILY'S PLACE OF worship from my memory to eighth grade (1960) was the Mt. Clinton Mennonite Church in Mt. Clinton, Virginia. Mt. Clinton was one of the first Valley Mennonite church buildings constructed of brick and without separate entrances for men and women, but after entering through a single entrance, the men and boys sat in the left pews while the women and girls sat on the right. The front "amen corners" on each side, with the pews turned at right angles to the others, were occupied by the oldest men and women respectively. I suppose those front angular pews were called the amen corners because if an "amen" in support of the preacher's words were heard, it likely came from the oldsters seated there.

Many, if not most, men wore a plain suit coat with a Nehru-style collar and no necktie. Women had their long un-cut hair up in a bun topped with a white "covering" or head veil. Most women wore cape dresses—specifically designed to de-emphasize their figures and keep any fancy embellishments at bay. The cape was similar to a vest in that it covered a woman from the waist up, with no sleeves; a piece of fabric with no pleats or frills, matching the fabric of the dress. If you met a Mennonite couple on the street in the nineteen-forties and fifties, and they were dressed in something other than their Sunday-go-to-meeting clothes, you would recognize the woman immediately as Mennonite because of the black bonnet on her head atop her covering or white prayer veil, and her plain dress, along with the black stockings and low heeled shoes. The man would likely look no different than other men, except perhaps a more conservative black hat. This disparity as to attire—the man looking normal, the woman anything but—made no sense to me then, and it still doesn't when I see conservative Mennonites, or those of other faiths, where females are required to wear distinctive religious attire in public while the men are not.

As late as 1955, the Virginia Mennonite Conference approved a resolution requiring specified attire for Sunday school officers and teachers, and in 1957, it re-affirmed the expectation of the plain coat for men and the covering, or head veil, along with the cape dress for women. That doesn't mean everyone in the congregation followed this admonition. But we all knew that "those folks" who did not wear regulation garb were very unlikely to be candidates for any church office or position. Uncut hair for women and not wearing jewelry or wedding rings remained a test for communion and membership through at least the late nineteen-fifties. Men seemed less constrained by Conference actions compared to women, and by 1960, neckties were much more ubiquitous. In fact, after conceding that my oldest brother, Dan, could wear a tie to fit in at the Virginia School for the Blind where he attended, my Dad found it difficult to hold the line with the rest of us boys. First, brother Eldon bought a tie at the Farm Bureau store in Harrisonburg, then later that same week brother Jim and I found our ties at the Penny's Department Store located on the town square. Eldon and I selected reasonably conservative dark colored ties. Jim, on the other hand, came home with a bright red one. After what seems with hindsight to have been hours of practice on Saturday learning to tie the knot, Eldon and I wore our neckties to church that Sunday. Jim had to go tieless until the following week, Dad having insisted on an exchange of the red tie. Eldon made all three of us tie clips out of strips of aluminum; made fancy by putting a lead pencil in an electric drill and using the eraser to create circular images on the face of the shiny aluminum. We wore those clips with pride.

Churches have always experienced the stress of negotiating a way forward that balances the need to be faithful to their past while trying to gain relevancy in an ever-changing larger culture. For example, in mainline Protestant denominations in the twenty-first century, a prominent issue has been homosexuality. However, for the Mennonite Church in the Shenandoah Valley in the nineteen-fifties and early nineteen-sixties, issues of appearance, or appropriate dress, were a vital element of the faith, and provided an element of stress that increased as the years passed. After 1960 when our family began attending Weavers Mennonite Church, for reasons I will explain later, the momentum for change quickened in the church. However, it met continuing resistance in our home. In high school gym class, I had to wear full-length blue jeans instead of regulation gym shorts. We were expected to take our gym clothes home each Friday for laundry. I carefully wrapped mine in the towel so those on the bus could not see the blue jeans, or so I hoped.

Of course, wearing dresses was still the norm for all females during regular class sessions. But Mennonite girls' dresses were plainer, even for those not yet wearing cape dresses. A Mennonite girl wearing shorts for any reason, in public at least, simply did not happen. I remember the girl who sat at the desk across from me in sixth grade telling me she was wearing red shorts under her skirt. Just the thought of a girl in shorts, much less the sight, was—shall we say—outside the norm for this Mennonite boy. Then, to prove it, she pulled up her skirt.

I was startled one Sunday morning at Weavers Mennonite Church to see a couple, recently married, walk into the service wearing wedding rings. It was shocking! And they sat together instead of following the customary "males to the left and females to the right" pattern, as some bold souls were beginning to do. The couple came back the next week still wearing rings. They had not been excommunicated. Equally shocking was attending a Mennonite Youth Convention in Ontario, Canada, as a high school student and discovering there were Mennonite girls from other places in the U.S. and Canada who had short hair and no coverings. Wow! That was mind boggling, exciting new data for me.

Acceptable Lifestyles

Lifestyle issues were also very much part of what it meant to be a good Mennonite in the Valley throughout my growing up years. Participating in dances, going to movies, and playing pool were prohibited. In seventh grade when dancing lessons were part of physical education class, I had to go to the library instead.

Living a plain life extended beyond plain attire to a non-showy style of living. Our car was as plain as one could buy—no whitewall tires, nor two tone paint. We kept the house and barn painted and in good repair—but that was to preserve the siding and roof, not for show. If I heard it once, I heard it a thousand times from Dad, "Pride goeth before destruction, a haughty spirit before a fall." It was my fifth-grade teacher who gave me a fresh perspective. She was encouraging us to take pride in our work and our appearance. She said with considerable conviction, "Someone who has no pride is worse than a jelly fish, just wishy-washy, without a backbone." Her stance made much more sense to me than my Dad's oft-repeated admonition. It was one small change in understanding, but a large crack in my identification with Dad's world view.

Another lifestyle issue related to insurance. A Conference resolution in 1953 drew the line against members carrying any insurance that would provide a lump sum payment in the event of loss. However, the sharing of some forms of loss within the Brotherhood was permitted, in fact, encouraged, with the establishment of a formal Mennonite Property Aid Plan and an Automobile Aid

Plan. However, when my mother and oldest brother spent considerable time in the hospital in the early nineteen-fifties, we had no health insurance. Without the financial support of a neighbor, our family ship might have sunk. If the church family came to our financial assistance during that time, I was never aware of it. But that could have been because of Dad's proclivity toward silence in matters of family finance as related to how much money came in, from where, or how it was spent. We just heard there was no extra money to spend, and I am sure that was true.

Even during those tough times, and continuing after that, my dad found his way to "care for those in need" while "not letting the right hand know what the left hand was doing." His contribution to the offering plate on Sunday mornings was always a wadded up bill, the denomination of which I never knew. But folks in need, especially those folks from further back toward the mountains, or one of his younger brothers, were his true ministry. It was not uncommon to see one of their cars meander up the driveway. Dad would slip outside to talk. Often we'd see him reach into the top pocket of his bid overalls, retrieve his wallet, and offer cash. We knew things would be tighter than usual until the next monthly milk check arrived. One experience, in particular, stays with me. I had stayed home from school for some reason, but I must not have been that sick. It was mid-December. At noon, Dad asked me to take some envelopes to the mailbox before the carrier arrived. While walking down our gravel lane, I held the envelopes up to the sun, trying to see what was inside. To my surprise, each contained a check made out in amounts that made me gasp. But he never, ever talked about his generosity. Dad was truly egalitarian in his regard for others, with a singular regard for those less fortunate than ourselves. This understanding of how to treat others has remained with me over the years.

A television set was definitely on the list of items that were worldly and prohibited. My parents never had one in their house as long as they lived. When my wife and I got married, my parents gave us money as a wedding gift. Was it poetic justice that we used some of their money to buy a small black and white TV? My catching up as an adult on *The Andy Griffith* and *Lawrence Welk* shows did not always sit well with my wife and kids who preferred other, more current shows. I don't remember not having a radio growing up in Dad's house. Regular fare in the morning was Witt Robinson on WSVA, but I also remember Dad's admonition to turn it off if he heard pop music or sporting events. Brother Jim seemed to have the knack of keeping the volume down just low enough and going off in a corner somewhere so he could listen to baseball games. After years of attempting to hold the line, the Conference finally gave up its prohibition against radios in 1954. This sudden "no to yes" reversal is particularly ironic in that soon thereafter, the Conference became a leader in radio Ministries with Mennonite Broadcasts, Incorporated.

The only non-church magazine that came into our house on a regular basis was *Readers Digest*. I read it from cover to cover, especially the section about new or unusual words. I resolved to use as many of those words as I could in the coming weeks. One day after reading that section, I was taking a shortcut across the lawn to the gravel lane to meet the school bus. I stopped on the bank by the peony bushes and resolved to stop using the word "ain't." I kept that sixth grade resolution for years, discovering later in life that sometimes, for emphasis, in a board or staff meeting, "ain't" seemed the perfect word. We also subscribed to the local daily paper. If you "snuck off" to another room, you could read the comics without reprimand. Getting caught reading a comic book was a serious infraction.

A core element of Mennonite life meant a commitment to, and lifestyle of, non-resistance or pacifism. Mennonites have a long history of opposition to war and to participation in the military, in any way, over hundreds of years. Many paid a high price for adhering to their conscience on these matters. One way this played out in our household was a prohibition against any toy guns. We did have an old twelve gauge shotgun, and later Dad purchased Jim and me a single shot twenty-two caliber rifle. But, oh how I yearned, as a youngster, for my own belt, holster, and cap gun. The best we could do was fashion our toy rifles and pistols out of wood in the farm shop. But we only played with them in the barn, never bringing them into the house.

I had a mixed experience with non-resistance. On one occasion, as a ninth grader, I was needling my seat mate on the school bus about a girl. He turned and popped me right on the nose with his fist. I knew I could have taken him, but instead, I just sucked it up and did not hit back; the parental admonition we'd often heard to "turn the other cheek" held sway. On an earlier occasion, while in fifth grade, I took a different path. While waiting for the bus ride home after school, another student picked on me. I'd had it with him. I pummeled him to the ground and kicked him for good measure. He screamed and began crying—perhaps just to attract attention. Fortunately, a group of other students partially hid us from the principal's view. I could see the principal start walking up the incline toward us to investigate. I slipped off to the side and quickly jumped on the bus, praying that the driver would drive off before the principal figured things out. He did. A robust adherence to our non-resistance position also kept me from accepting the honor I received in high school of being selected to attend Boy's State. Permission was denied because Boy's State was sponsored by a military-related organization. The second and third choices for Boy's State that year were also from Mennonite families—all declined, so no one attended from our school that year.

Tobacco use and alcohol consumption were also prohibited in my childhood, though both had been common among Mennonites in an earlier century in the Valley. My first experience with both did not unduly hasten my desire to use tobacco or imbibe. Normally, with a last name beginning with the letter "B," my seat was at or near the front of the class. However in seventh grade, I sat in a back row desk. One day another student brought a can of snuff he had taken from his father's pants. It was not his first time. For me, it was my first and last experience with snuff—ever! And a few years later, my cousin and I were biking around Silver Lake in Dayton, Virginia, when we found an unopened beer bottle left behind by late night partiers. It was warm from lying in the sun.

I thought it tasted like cow piss. Later in life, though, I enjoyed a pipe for some years and still enjoy the fruits of the vine.

Any lifestyle that involved divorce and remarriage was outside the bounds of Mennonite life in the Valley all through this time. No one who was divorced or remarried could be a member of a Virginia Conference Mennonite Church. And marrying outside the faith, especially a Catholic, was anathema. When my older brother married a Catholic girl, two of my aunts—my father's sisters—raised a considerable clamor about it. How could this happen in the Bowman family? There is justice in this world, proven later when both aunts had sons who married Catholic girls.

Another often heard phrase at home was about being "unequally yoked." By 1950, the Conference made little reference to it, but in earlier decades it was of great concern. It applied to, and prohibited, things such as membership in the Farm Bureau, the Rotary Club, secret societies, or any joint stock companies if any of the owners were non-Mennonites. The issue of being unequally yoked also applied to political office, with a prohibition against holding any prominent civil office. Post office work and participation on local school boards were granted exceptions. For us children, this was just another reason we could not participate in extracurricular activities at school. Of course, we also had farm chores that took precedence over any school activities. That meant waking at 4:30 A.M. during summer months and 5:00 A.M. in the winter to milk and feed the cows and to tend the turkeys. Two hours of chores each morning and evening, before and after school, was the norm.

Church Practice and Polity

Perhaps more important, or at least more substantive, in some people's minds than issues of apparel and lifestyle, were issues of church practice and polity. A communion service, with the traditional bread and grape juice instead of wine, was held twice a year. Had it occurred more often would it have been less memorable? Perhaps. Communion for us also meant foot washing and the holy kiss. Children did not participate in communion until they were baptized and joined the church, typically in early teen years. Observing baptisms and communion as a young child in no way prepared me for the events when I first took part. Along with others, I was baptized and then participated in my first communion during the same worship service.

Other than the water running down my forehead, off the tip of my nose, and piddling on the floor, the baptism itself was no big deal. It was the holy kiss that followed baptism which unnerved me. In Valley Mennonite churches at the time, after baptism, males were received into the church with a kiss full on the mouth by any ministers or bishops involved in the service. Females were greeted similarly by the ministers' and bishops' wives. The kiss itself was shocking enough, but the stench of bad breath that came with it was unbearable.

My first communion followed my baptism. It was the morsel of bread followed by a sip of grape juice from a shared cup. And the ministers did not pretend to turn the cup around or wipe the cup's edge between sips. After communion, the males washed feet in the front of the church, while the ladies went to the privacy of the Sunday school rooms in the back. Washing feet meant pairing up with another person, sitting on chairs opposite each other, with a basin of water on the floor between and a towel on one's knee. Each person, in turn, bent over to "wash" and dry the other's feet. Then the two would stand and follow the holy kiss protocol. The bishop who baptized me was my first foot washing partner, and I experienced for a second time in one day that same awful breath.

That first communion, foot washing, and holy kiss experience left me with a permanent scar. And things got even worse a year or two later. A non-Mennonite family occasionally attended Mt. Clinton Mennonite Church. The family was, shall we say, from back towards the mountains. One son was a classmate of mine at Mt. Clinton Elementary School. He had taken to making snarky remarks to other students at my school on Monday about the strange goings-on at the Mennonite Church on Sundays prior. When communion and foot washing time rolled around, he was in the pew directly behind me. I'll never forget his outburst, "Jesus

Christ! They're washing feet in church!" I knew it was going to be a rough Monday morning at school the next day.

In earlier days, the communion service was preceded by church members meeting privately, during the week prior, with a minister, a practice referred to as council meetings. In this meeting, each member was queried as to any lurking known or hidden sin that needed to be confessed so the member could commune with integrity. One vivid memory, from Mt. Clinton Church, of the results of this activity remains with me. How the ministers determined what sins merited public confession in front of God and the whole congregation, I have no idea, but, obviously, some sins reached that threshold. In the worship service, before communion, and at the minister's prodding, a guy stood up with his ill-fated wife by his side and confessed to having "laid" with another woman. Their children cowered in the pew beside them. I knew, even at my tender age, there was something terribly wrong about this.

I have no doubt the practice and imagery of foot washing, perhaps even the holy kiss, is meaningful to some, but I felt traumatized by it. The holy kiss eventually died of its own accord, but not before I figured out how to step around foot washing and the accompanying holy kiss when we began attending Weavers Mennonite Church. Because of a difference in the design of the building, the men at Weavers got up from their pews row by row and walked in a line to the back anterooms where they engaged in foot washing, paired off with the person directly in front or behind them in the line. Then one would walk out the other side and return to their pew. Well, I would walk to the back—and just keep walking ever so slowly. My place in line would be filled by the person behind me—and I would walk out the other side and return to my pew, never having stopped for foot washing or the concluding holy kiss. Looking back, I recognize this as another significant crack in my understanding of the church and its control, or lack thereof, over my life when feeling less than whole from something the church expected.

From its beginning in the seventeenth century, Mennonite Church ministers were selected and ordained by "lot" and were expected to be "tent maker" preachers, meaning they earned their living in addition to preaching. A person's own sense of being "called" to the ministry was not a factor in selection; it was calling by the church through the lot that mattered. Formal seminary training was viewed with suspicion by many, including my Dad, even after a Mennonite seminary was established in conjunction with Eastern Mennonite College in 1965. While not compensated with any salary, ministers did receive periodic love offerings or support in the form of help with their spring planting or fall harvest. In response, no doubt, to rising expectations of the role of ministers, a Conference resolution in 1950 noted that ministers who gave more time than had been expected in the past should be given more support. However this was followed by a statement that it was not a call in favor of a "commercialized, corrupted ministry." I remember a note in a Weavers Church bulletin sometime in the early nineteen-sixties where-in both ministers thanked the congregation for the gift of financial support they had received from a dedicated offering that had been announced as "in support of the ministers." When you think about it, that kind of offering is about as direct a means as one can employ for indicating support, or lack thereof, for the minister. I have never forgotten a friend— a minister's son—who confided that they got used tea bags on a regular basis from one parishioner.

Spoken prayer in any church service was a male prerogative, exclusively. In fact, any man could be called upon to pray in any service, without prior warning. On the few occasions when Dad was called on, I experienced a flash of anxiety, worrying that he might say something that would elicit laughter from the other boys. One embarrassing episode stands out in my mind when the man called upon—not my Dad—simply failed to perform. Debate followed among us boys as to whether he had not heard his name or just refused. After a time of silence, the minister said "amen." No prayers were written out, but those who prayed on a regular basis had a recognizable prayer protocol. No written liturgies were used, and no sermons were scripted. In fact, at one time the Conference had passed a prohibition against written sermons, believing doing so got in the way of allowing the spirit to speak in the moment. During congregational prayers, attendees were expected to rise partly, turn, and kneel in the pew. There were no forward kneelers like in Catholic churches. Considerable age and/or excessive girth were acceptable excuses from this prayer protocol. As we reached the age when we could sit with our friends instead of with our fathers, we boys found kneeling for prayer a great time for extra-curricular activities, things like note passing or flipping pennies. I almost never won when flipping coins, an experience that taught me more about the ills of gambling than any sermon or Sunday school admonition.

The Great Awakening and Great Revival movements of the late 1700s and early 1800s, respectively, were not supported by most Mennonites, and certainly not by Mennonite Church leadership. Some who sought greater emotional expression transitioned to other churches, but the Mennonite Church did not endorse any form of "revival" in those early years. During the first half of the twentieth century, there was considerable push and pull in the Mennonite Church related to revival or what some called extended services. However, the revivals I remember were when George Brunk II brought his big truck and revival tent to the Valley in the nineteen-fifties. The Brunk revival, set up at the Rockingham County Fairgrounds in 1954, is as fresh in my mind today as when it happened. The tent seemed huge with side curtains, long support poles, bright flood lights strung along the peak, rows of folding metal chairs, and walkways surfaced in fresh sawdust or wood chips. Hell fire and brimstone preaching were intermixed with group a cappella singing. When the time came toward the end of the service for the altar call, the song leader led in a soft, but intense, rendition of "Just as I Am." Between verses of the song, the evangelist pleaded with any sinners to come to the front to be saved. Dad made clear our attendance was obligatory. Looking back, that is somewhat surprising, given my father's discomfort with any emotional expression of religious fervor, but Dad greatly respected George Brunk II. The threat of eternal damnation scared me to death, even as a second grader going on third grader, but I was not ready to join the church. I tightly gripped the sides of my chair with sweat stained fingers, ensuring I did not stand and walk forward. Later, when I was a young teenager, Dad volunteered me to help set up the revival tent. The volunteer foreman gave me a large sledge hammer and told me to drive stakes for the restraining ropes. After breaking two sledge hammer handles, I was relieved of duty.

The use of musical instruments was a particularly vexing problem over time for the church. Use of musical instruments in any church service was always prohibited, but at one point, leadership requested that all members destroy or dispose of any musical instruments at home. Doing so was traumatic for many families. An older first cousin of mine remembers her father destroying a reed organ that was the pride and joy of her mother. By the nineteen-sixties, the use of musical instruments at home was no longer an issue. In fact, soon after the Conference officially changed its position in 1947, Dad bought an old reed organ and brought it home. Later we had a piano, and my older siblings remember Dad playing both the organ and piano. I was puzzled that music lessons were OK for my brother Dan, who was blind, but other siblings who wanted to learn were not given support. I made one aborted attempt on my own at learning to play the guitar. It was simply not my gift.

Four-part, a cappella congregational singing was the norm in church, something that when well done still transports me to higher ground. Even though the Conference in 1940 took a determined stand against special music in morning worship services, hence no church choirs, small groups such as quartets were very popular for evening services and special meetings. One of my most prominent memories is of my Dad singing first tenor in a men's quartet for over forty-five years. When younger, I considered it a treat to ride along with the quartet for its evening presentation because normally there would be space for only one, or maybe two, additional passengers. Amos Rhodes, a fellow quartet member, did wear a tie, the only quartet member not to wear a plain coat, and he was allowed to lead congregational singing at Mt. Clinton Mennonite Church. I guess there are exceptions to all rules, an observation I made early on. I was puzzled that Dad seemed to accept, without condemnation, unsanctioned behavior in what seemed to me to be a selected few, but not others, and certainly not that same defiant behavior in his children. I guess as children we are all highly tuned to any shreds of evidence of what we perceive as inconsistency or hypocrisy.

Sunday school was just another part of Sunday life during my growing up years. I had no idea how controversial it had been in years prior in the Mennonite Church. At Mt. Clinton, I remember Sunday school as a time to be with near-age friends but little else. It was while attending Sunday school at Weavers that the thought began to form in my mind that perhaps Sunday school was simply a place where the teacher shared his ignorance, and we all departed with greater shared ignorance. It seemed a rote recitation of prescribed protocol from the Sunday school booklet rather than any serious study or inquiry. On occasion, a well thought out, but out of the box, question from a student, to which the teacher could only recite the standard scriptural citation, drove that point home.

Another one of those earlier Valley Mennonite controversies, but one that had become readily accepted by my time at Mt. Clinton, was Vacation Bible School. It was two weeks of morning classes, held at the church, beginning the week after the school year closed. Most of the attendees were fellow church goers, but invariably some community children participated. We would line up outside by class and then sing "We are Marching to Zion" as we entered the building. Vacation Bible School left me, to this day, with a major regret. We would also line up inside at the front of the church mid-morning for group singing. While not musically gifted, I can sing once songs have become familiar to me. It was the summer after fourth grade. By that time, I was very much aware of my Dad's discomfort with the primary minister and some of his "progressive" ideas for the congregation, all of which contributed to our family's move several years later from Mt. Clinton to Weavers Mennonite Church. Once, when I stood to sing, along with the other children, I assertively refused to open my mouth. The minister asked if I didn't want to learn to sing, to which I replied, "No!" Looking back as an adult, I now realize I would unquestionably side with that minister's progressive attitudes rather than parrot my Dad's positions. But at the time, I thought I was supportive of Dad in being non-cooperative. I would like a do-over on that one. I mentioned the minister's progressive agenda. One of the troubling issues for my Dad was the minister's promotion of adding a fellowship hall. The church had none, and some, including my Dad, were convinced it should stay that way. After all, churches were for worship, not fun and games.

While I don't remember ministers talking about it from the pulpit, the issue of race relations still simmered on occasion. The Conference took a stand against segregation in 1953, but not everyone's heart followed suit. One member of Dad's quartet expressed his angst about the Conference decision while traveling in the car to a service one Sunday evening. My Dad politely but firmly told him that his views supportive of segregation had no biblical basis. It didn't change his mind, but I was proud of my Dad that night and still respect him for his views on this matter.

Women were forbidden any leadership role in the church, except for exclusive female activities such as a ladies Sunday school class. The protocol that women could not facilitate any activity that included both men and women was a policy and practice my Dad whole heartedly supported. In fact, the topic of a woman's place in the church, and in the home, was covered on a regular basis from the head of our table at mealtimes. Even in his later years, when a prominent Mennonite minister was brought up on charges of inappropriate relationships with multiple women, my Dad was convinced the women involved were the instigators. My Dad always liked and respected the secondary minister at Mt. Clinton. This minister's wife hosted a prominent program on Mennonite Broadcasts. I could sense Dad's discomfort with this, but I do not remember any negative comments about her work, another one of those "exceptions" I suppose.

Looking back, it strikes me as amazing that we grew up very much aware of discussion about various end time scenarios. In fact, differences of opinion on this matter caused one of the deepest schisms among faculty in the history of Eastern Mennonite

School. I never saw it as having any practical significance for my life, but it was one of those things that early on led me to question the energy and passion with which some engage in petty theological discourse. For me, the debate among the premillennialists, the postmillennialists, and the amillennialists ranked right up there with the question of how many angels could dance on the head of a pin as an absolutely absurd theological conundrum. As a practical matter, everyone in the church that I knew expected the second coming soon, most likely in their lifetime. As happens periodically, a self-proclaimed "prophet" in the community announced that Christ was coming back to earth on a given Sunday—and he was to arrive at the Mt. Clinton Mennonite Church Cemetery at the break of dawn. We heard on WSVA radio that the prophet and his followers had gathered at the cemetery well before sunrise to meet Jesus as he arrived in the air. By the time we arrived at the church that Sunday morning, it was apparent the prophet had misheard or miscalculated. Dad was certainly not supportive of anyone knowing the time and place, but he fully expected Christ's return soon.

Normally, politics and religion were not overtly mixed in my father's pontifications. We were admonished that there were two kingdoms, the kingdom of heaven and the kingdom of this world. Our allegiance and focus were to be with the kingdom of heaven, which meant that affairs of this world were not consequential. Accordingly I did not grow up hearing debate about Republicans versus Democrats or discussions around the dinner table about politics generally or other affairs of the kingdom of man. The presidential election in 1960 presented an exception. Dad believed a victory by Kennedy would mean rule by Catholics and the Pope, and that was more than worrisome, perhaps even one of those symbols of the end time.

5

Mennonites, Their Anabaptist
Heritage, and Me

I HAVE TALKED ABOUT the Virginia Conference Mennonite Church
in the Valley as I experienced it in my father's house on a personal
and practical basis. It will be helpful in relating my story onward
to give readers a very brief overview of the theology and origins
of Mennonites. Their heritage traces back to the Anabaptists who
were part of the radical Reformation in Europe in the seventeenth
century. Anabaptist leaders took the position that Martin Luther
and other reformers had not gone far enough with their reforms.
Anabaptists rejected infant baptism, insisting instead on adult
baptism, believing that being a Christian was a decision to be made
voluntarily by adults. They also refused to participate in any military activities and refused the taking of oaths, in general, saying
that one's allegiance must be to God, not to men. While passively
obeying the civil government, they declined to participate in holding civil offices. They believed in a gathered, voluntary church—
not a territorial or state sponsored church. Discipleship was vital,
with a literal understanding of the Sermon on the Mount as the
core of Christian ethics and practice. Scripture alone was the final
authority. A simple life in all aspects was also considered essential
to a life of faith. The name "Mennonite" comes from the name

"Menno Simons," one of the most prominent early leaders. The Mennonites who began arriving as immigrants in Pennsylvania in the early 1700s were often referred to as "Mennonists."

Anabaptists did share with other Protestant faiths a belief in the triune God, in the saving work of Jesus on the cross, and in the hope of life eternal with God for those faithful to his word. Those who refused would spend eternity in hell. Women wore the covering or head veil as a sign of submission to the God ordained headship of a woman to man, man to Christ, and Christ to God.

Without a doubt, the Mennonite Church I experienced had been influenced by tenants of fundamentalism as espoused by the Moody Bible Institute and other "non-Mennonite but very fundamentalist promoting" entities in the late 1800s and early 1900s. Anabaptist Mennonites were persecuted by both Catholics and Protestants. While always claiming to remain Anabaptist and "neither Catholic nor Protestant," still when forced by the fundamentalist debate in the early 1900s to choose, most Mennonites came down on the side of Protestant fundamentalism. For Valley Mennonites, George Brunk I, father of evangelist George Brunk II, and J.L. Stauffer probably get most of the credit—or blame—for stalwartly advocating fundamentalist tenants, which were an integral part of the religion of my Dad, and hence of my childhood and youth.

So my experience was traditional Anabaptist Mennonite, with a smattering of fundamentalism, but there was something more in that religious stew.

6

Appalachian Mountain Religion

I MENTIONED ABOVE THAT the religion I rejected was primarily the religion of the Virginia Mennonite Conference churches in the Valley in the nineteen-fifties and early nineteen-sixties, with a hint of Appalachian mountain religion. What is, or was, Appalachian mountain religion? I was very much aware while growing up, of a distinct culture among those who lived further back towards the mountains. I did not see myself and our family as part of that culture, but it was close at hand. I don't recall, growing up, that we used the words "Hill" or "Mountain" culture as distinct from a Valley culture, but we were certainly aware of the distinction. It was not until much later that I came to appreciate the distinction fully, and to realize how both are part and parcel of who I am today.

I always felt some tension between Dad and some of Mom's family. We spent far more time with our Bowman relatives and cousins than with the Wenger side of our family. It began to dawn on me that my Dad's father's family was considered by many in the Valley to be Hill folks. My father's father, whose family had been Lutheran over generations, married a girl, my grandmother, who was deeply steeped in long-standing Mennonite tradition and Valley culture. My Grandmother Bowman set the religious tone in my Dad's growing up household. My Grandfather Bowman never wore the plain coat and stopped attending services as he aged. But all eleven of their children, including my Dad, grew up being very Mennonite, including wearing attire as sanctioned by the Conference.

When Dad left home soon after turning twenty-one years of age, he spent four years before he married living with his grandfather's family in a Hill culture area of Rockingham County, working for shares on his grandfather's farm. I know that experience gave Dad a lasting appreciation and respect for his Hill culture heritage, and I suspect it also gave him his first real experience with, and appreciation for, Appalachian mountain religion. After four years, Dad married a girl, my mother, from the Valley who had deep Mennonite roots. My Dad acknowledged to me once that he always felt inferior to others. I was shocked to hear him say it and equally shocked that I had not intuited it. It helped me better understand my own father. I used to say that I wanted my tombstone to read, "Here lies Bernie Bowman, the equal of any man but better than none." What was the Appalachian culture and Appalachian mountain religion that was part of my Dad's heritage?

For anyone interested in learning more about Appalachian mountain religion, I refer you to Deborah Vansau McCauley's book *Appalachian Mountain Religion: A History*. For my purposes here, the following few comments about Appalachian mountain religion will suffice. Most congregations do not relate to any centralized organization, and most follow a very literal interpretation of the Bible, typically the King James Version. Most adherents place great importance on religious experience—especially in relation to conversion. Life is seen and experienced as extremely hard; a person can only rely on oneself. They are reluctant to use professional pastors or send their preachers for seminary training, fearing corruption. They tend to be viewed by others as powerless, living in poverty—fitting subjects for saving, both from their sins and from their dire living conditions. A favorite hymn, "Further Along," is reflective of their understanding of the world and their position in it. They use terms like "not being proud and puffed up." They see charity properly done as more important than knowledge. "Knowledge puffeth up, but charity edifieth," as stated in I Corinthians. They speak of a broken heart, tenderness of heart, a heart that is not hardened to the spirit and to the word of God. The heart guides the head, not vice versa. "God laid it on my heart" is an everyday expression of their experience. They tend toward pietism; religious experience is a blessing. One cannot make a decision for Christ; one can only be open to the experience of saving grace in one's life. One is called and qualified to preach by God, not by education. The Bible is primary, and there is a real passion for simplicity and humility.

Keep these thoughts about Appalachian mountain religion as a backdrop as I relate added thoughts about my Father.

7

Continuing Journey with My Father

MY OLDEST BROTHER, DAN, remembers family life with adequate financial resources, a father actively involved in, and supportive of, church activities, and our Dad's participation in his children's play by crafting an assortment of toys and playthings. About the time I began school in 1952, Dad faced a series of financial and family challenges that would have broken most people. At the age of forty-eight, with eight children, and very soon after finally achieving his life-long dream of buying his own farm, my Dad had to cope with the financial and emotional burden of major medical catastrophes afflicting both his wife and his oldest son. Plus one end of his recently purchased barn collapsed, immediately after having been filled with freshly baled hay. There was no insurance to cover any of these losses. On top of all these unexpected expenses, he had farm mortgage payments to meet. Looking back, I certainly cannot fault him for not being as involved in my play as he had been earlier with my older siblings. He was just hanging on, trying to survive. I marvel that he accomplished that.

At about this same time, in the mid-nineteen-fifties, Dad began a journey of estrangement from Valley Mennonite life—after he had worked so hard to fit into that life. I suspect it was Dad's feelings of inferiority that had earlier compelled him to double down on trying to be the best Mennonite possible. The father I remember was no longer involved as he had been earlier. I never knew the father who had participated fully as a younger adult in things like singing schools, Sunday schools, and Vacation Bible Schools. He had even been in the lot, once for the office of deacon and later for minister. All these things were "progressive" for Valley Mennonites in Dad's younger adult years. Even the influx and influence of fundamentalism, which we do not see as progressive today, was progressive at that time for Valley Mennonite churches in that it was something new coming from outside the Mennonite heritage, being espoused and promoted by folks associated with Eastern Mennonite School. I never knew that progressive parent.

I am confident Dad's unexpected financial and family challenges contributed to his withdrawal from church activities, plus he apparently had a moment of self-reflection when one of my older brothers commented on all the time he spent on church functions rather than with his family. But without a doubt, during my grade school years, Dad's estrangement was aided and abetted by the very church he knew and loved in that it continued evolving or transitioning, but in ways that were uncomfortable, even unbiblical and sinful to him. There was movement away from the "bench" of alternating preachers to an assigned "pastor" for a given congregation. There was even movement toward paying the pastor instead of expecting him to be self-supporting. Women were becoming expressive about a fuller role in church life. There was serious talk of fellowship halls. What started like the proverbial camel's nose under the tent must have seemed to him a flood of sinful intrusions. The plain coat for men and the cape dress for women were fast disappearing. And then wedding rings began to appear, along with cut hair for women. Even the covering or head veil began to disappear. Mennonite women in the Valley were no longer easily distinguishable from the worldly folks around them. And there was talk of pledging instead of free-will offerings; and about the need for the congregation to develop and live by a budget. My Dad had found meaning and comfort in some of the "progressive" goings-on of Valley Mennonite churches in the first half of the twentieth century, but what some saw as continuing progress in the nineteen-fifties through the nineteen-seventies did not resonate with him at all. My Dad never put on a tie. During his later years, he was the only man still wearing the plain coat at Weavers Church. Perhaps it was his way of saying, "I am still true to the church that was, not to the church as it has become."

At one time in his life, Dad had made yeoman's efforts to be part of that Valley Mennonite Church community, but it moved away from him and in some ways rejected him. There is the story of a time when Dad was in the lot for calling of a new minister. A sister-in-law went to the bishops and expressed her view that Dad did not meet the qualifications to be in the lot. Another time, when he was overwhelmed by financial and family challenges, he found that his minister told a group of his fellow church members that "they needed to pray for Millard because he is slipping." And when Dad voiced his determination to buy his own farm, having lived all his growing up years as a tenant farmer's son, a prominent church member told him that he should abandon his dream. After all, some folks are ordained by God to be land owners, others to work the land for them. These experiences would cause any of us to wonder who was friend or foe. Perhaps it is no surprise I'd often hear him singing his two favorite hymns, "Further Along" and "Whispering Hope," both pleas of the oppressed longing for justice in some future haven.

Another story from the murky past may help explain Dad's views on education, which so impacted me. Dad left school after ninth grade to work on his father's dairy farm. That was more common than not among Mennonites at the time. However, someone must have recognized Dad as having real promise as a student. The story is that someone associated with Eastern Mennonite School, as it was known at the time, suggested that Dad consider running away from home so he could continue his studies. It seems this one educated person's misdirected advice colored Dad's view of education for his lifetime, an effect that I felt most directly in his being so opposed to my going to college. Dad did adopt his own path to self-education. He purchased a set of used encyclopedias, which he read volume by volume, through the entire set. I think it is fair to say, reading that encyclopedia was his evening TV watching.

Dad, who as a child and young adult had entirely bought into his mother's Mennonite religion and traditions, later became increasingly estranged from Valley Mennonite-dom; then he began a transition more toward some aspects of Appalachian mountain religion. However, one tenet of that religion never gained traction with him. He never, ever found comfort in any expressive, emotional display of religion as is often associated with Appalachian mountain religion. He did find his place with many of the other tenets, in particular, the primacy of the Bible literally interpreted; a fear of an educated ministry; a focus on practical Christian ethics and living; and, a focus on humility and low key charity.

I greatly value and emulate Dad's sense of egalitarianism to this day, along with his giving of full measure, his love of neighbor as self, and his love of reading and storytelling. In fact, I consider Dad's greatest gift to me to be all the stories he told at bedtime, along with the books he would read to us. Little could he have known that the love of reading he instilled in me would provide me with a world and religious view so different from what he had promulgated.

8

Moving Past Childhood and Youth

Two Years Between High School and College

A FAMILY TRADITION WAS well in place by the time I came along. In their first winter following high school graduation, each of my older siblings attended a six-week winter session at Rosedale Bible School in Ohio, a Conservative Mennonite Conference affiliated institution. Keep in mind, in my Dad's world, children owed their parents their labor on the farm until they were twenty-one years of age. He had worked until he was twenty-one years old for his father. "Letting us go early" as he phrased it, at the age of twenty rather than twenty-one, was an act of generosity on his part; at least, he thought it so. This meant, for all of us, spending two years at home working on the farm after high school, with the exception of six weeks at Rosedale, before striking out on a life of our own. I attended Rosedale, perpetuating that family tradition. While I was not particularly comfortable with the theology espoused there, it was very pleasant for me. It was my first experience of a more serious study of the Bible and religion, an interest that stays with me to this day. I must also confess, it was wonderful not having to milk the cows or feed the turkeys during those cold winter weeks.

In keeping with Dad's rules, I worked at home on the farm for two years after graduation from high school. During that time, I joined a younger sister in attending Zion Hill Mennonite Church instead of Weavers. Zion Hill was one of those mission outreach congregations located at the base of the mountains. While Valley Mennonite in most respects, looking back I can see Zion Hill did have some of the Appalachian mountain religion flavor. No longer attending church with my parents was certainly a small step toward independence on my part. I found warm and welcoming people in that congregation. In fact, it was while attending Zion Hill that I became aware, consciously, of what I came to see more fully over time as perhaps the most redeeming feature, to me, of congregational life. That is, it's social function, a place of gathering and acceptance. In later church attendance, even as I became increasingly estranged from some tenets of the church, I was always able to find a group of like-minded folks with whom I could be comfortable, folks with whom I could discuss freely without rebuttal, platitudes, or pontification. Beginning to see the church in this way at Zion Hill was not intentional on my part, but a shift, none-the-less, away from thinking of the church as dogma and doctrine, a position I learned later to be where the Christian Church essentially began.

Those two years on the farm after high school only sharpened my desire to go to college. Even though several older siblings had attended college by this time, Dad's opposition to higher education remained strong. Had I chosen to stay on the farm, Dad would have been helpful in any way possible. In fact, in the summer before college was to start for me, the neighboring farm came up for sale. Dad indicated that he had talked with a banker, and if I stayed on the farm, he would buy that neighboring farm to ensure there would be adequate income for a two-generation farming operation. I declined the offer and reaffirmed my intention of attending college. I later discovered Dad told a neighbor he did not know what I was going to do that fall because he didn't think I had the money to go to college. In fact, this came after he refused to sign papers saying he would not provide any financial assistance so I could qualify for a financial aid package without any participation on his part. What Dad had not counted on was that one neighbor went to the bank and co-signed a loan for me; another offered a private loan to make up what additional I needed. As you can imagine, this was a significant break-a-way moment for me. When my Dad declined to be helpful to the life direction I had chosen, I found others more than willing to step in.

There was another significant happening in those two years. I can no longer recall the book's title or the author, but somehow I came into possession of a book about how the Bible came to be. This book described what was known from critical analysis of the Bible itself as well as from historical inquiry. Reading the book gave me a sense of wonder and understanding, intermixed with angst and discomfort at how far it took me from my upbringing. So the Bible did not come down from heaven verbatim in King James English to God's appointed scribes who merely wrote what they heard? And you mean the Catholic Bible contains books that are not in the Protestant Bible? How can that be? And are you telling me the books of the New Testament were not written until decades after Jesus had died, and there are discrepancies between the Gospel writers' accounts? The seeds of rising import for intellectual integrity and honesty in religion had been sown. As time went along, I found it increasingly difficult to be comfortable with any religious expression that did not give equal value to one's intellect, along with one's heart.

College and Two Papers

It was corn harvest time when I left home for college. For dairy farmers in the Valley that meant silo filling time, the shredding by a corn harvester of the entire corn stalk, ears and all, into silage, transported in wagons from the field and blown up into tall silos. I left home two weeks before my twentieth birthday, something Dad had pointed out to me as further evidence of his generosity. Even though the college was less than five miles from home, I did not even consider any living arrangement other than dorm life. I had a letter instructing me to show up for orientation at the dorm by 5:00 P.M. on the appointed day. We "filled silo" all that day and Dad said not a word about my leaving or how I might get to the dorm. I had no car of my own, so my only transportation was via Dad's car. At four o'clock I emptied the silage wagon I had brought in from the field, then pulled the tractor and wagon off to the side, went to the house, took a bath, loaded my clothes and my new alarm clock radio into Dad's Mercury and drove myself to school. My younger sisters were busy with chores so they could not take me. I told them they would have to figure out how to pick up the car at the dorm with the extra set of keys I left with them. I have said many times, it was only five miles down the road to college, but the world it opened up for me was the equivalent of going half way around the world.

A significant self-discovery early in my college experience was how much I both learned and found my own voice, to use a literary term, from the exercise of writing. I took copious notes in class, which I often could not read later because of my bad handwriting. But it seemed the act of writing planted the information in my brain. An interesting anecdote about my mother is that she took great pride in the excellent cursive she learned using the Palmer Method in school. My fifth-grade teacher, knowing of her desire that my handwriting improve, determined to help. Unfortunately, each six-week report card home included a note, "Bernard's handwriting has not improved." In this and following chapters, I highlight a variety of my previous writings in that these were points of significant discovery of my own voice.

At a very young age I knew I had a different perspective on religion and the world than that of my Dad. However, I was finding a way to get along within the Mennonite Church without "owning" Dad's views, perhaps because the Mennonite Church, itself, was fast evolving. It was moving rapidly away from the church my Dad had valued, toward new and more progressive positions. For some years, even as I moved into full adulthood, I found room to "leave Dad's church" but still find a place for myself in what the Mennonite Church was becoming, but not without some angst. Three experiences stand out for me from my college experience in this regard, perhaps in juxtaposition to each other; one while participating in a Junior Year Abroad program in Japan; two others upon my return as a senior to complete my degree at Eastern Mennonite College (now University).

Through the Council of Mennonite Colleges Junior Year Abroad Program I attended International Christian University (ICU) in Japan. Students came to ICU from all over the world bringing great cultural, but also religious, diversity. I had never experienced such diversity. For the first time in my life, folks would ask me if I was a Christian in the same way one might ask if I was American or from a given state within the United States. Growing up in the Valley, people did ask about denominational affiliation, but no one had asked if I was a Christian. That was assumed. I was surprised at the anxiety that question generated in me. I wanted to respond, "First, I need to know what your understanding of Christianity is, and then I can answer." You see, I knew by this time there were aspects and elements of Christianity, as practiced, that I did not want to be associated with. But at the same time, I was not completely rejecting of it either. One Shinto priest, sensing my awkwardness with his question, pursued a much more in-depth discussion with me. He said, "I understand your discomfort with Christianity. From my viewpoint, Christianity is a bloody religion based on human sacrifice. What kind of God would act like the Christian God? Telling a man in the Old Testament to kill his own son and then in the New Testament sending his son to die on a cross. It is a very, very strange religion for today's world." That was a perspective I had never, ever contemplated!

My experience with the Shinto priest in Japan came back to memory when years later I read a vignette from Joseph Campbell, famed scholar and author. He tells of an American theologian who after touring many Shinto shrines and observing their religious ceremonies, asked the Shinto priest—and I paraphrase, "I've seen your shrines and ceremonies, but I don't see or get your ideology or theology." Upon reflection, the priest responded, "I don't think we have ideology or theology. We dance!" What an expression of being joyfully alive! Is it not in those moments of truly being alive that our physical life resonates with our inner being, and what we feel is the rapture of being alive?

In my senior year at EMC, after my junior year abroad experience in Japan, I told my professor that I wanted to write my term paper about John Funk. I thought I was referring to the Funk who had lived in Singers Glen, Virginia, and who was instrumental in promoting music and singing in Valley churches in the 1800s, but I had misremembered this gentleman's name as John rather than Joseph. The professor was delighted, thinking I wanted to write about the John Funk who lived in Indiana and was a prominent leader in the Mennonite Church in the late nineteenth century. John Funk began a publishing company which became the Mennonite Publishing Company, with its signature publication being *Herald of Truth*. The professor provided me with me several good references for background material along with strong encouragement—so I decided not to tell him I had a different Funk in mind. The paper I wrote, "John F. Funk and the Revival Movement," won third place in the Mennonite Church Historical Committee's John Horsch Mennonite History Student Essay Contest for 1971/1972. It was published in the *Gospel Herald* on March 21, 1972, after which John Oyer, editor of the *Mennonite Quarterly Review*, asked me to do some additional research so the paper could be published in the *Review*. Unfortunately, I delayed and did not get that accomplished.

A second short piece I wrote while at EMC entitled "Is the Anabaptist Vision a Myth?" was also published, in the *Gospel Herald* in the September 11, 1973, issue. It was my first serious study of Mennonite Church history specifically focused on its Anabaptist beginnings. I found great empathy in the Anabaptist ideals of voluntary discipleship, a community of believers, and Sermon on the Mount ethics. While the pettiness of some of the issues over which the church was willing to divide seemed foolish to me, the distinctiveness and courage of those initial Anabaptists and their followers in attempting to carry out and live by those principles gave me a sense of pride in Mennonite Church tradition I had not previously experienced. This publication garnered me a quote in

Kauffman and Harder's *Anabaptists Four Centuries Later* volume, referring to me as a "spokesman for the younger generation."

With the benefit of hindsight and the insights borrowed recently from Robin Meyers, minister and author, I can better articulate what so caught my interest about my Anabaptist forefathers. Meyers presented the 2013–2014 Lyman Beecher Lecture at Yale Divinity School. A summary of this lecture was published in The Jesus Seminar's publication, *The Fourth R*, November-December 2015 edition. Meyers never mentions the Anabaptists, but what he says is spot on for them. He speaks of " . . . the cause of death of the church today as caused largely by pseudo-followers of Jesus who are indistinguishable from the dominant culture." He continues as follows:

> Why not make the case that the Bible itself is a manifesto of resistance and that no renewal of the church is possible until the Beloved Community abandons nostalgia and modern purity codes and becomes subversive in its resistance to the forces of death in our time? . . . Whatever else may be said of the Jesus Movement, it was born in opposition to the status quo. Now it largely sanctifies the status quo. Its founder constituted an unacceptable risk to the Roman Empire, and that resistance seemed so counter-intuitive and subversive that even his mental health was questioned. . . . Faith is not so much about believing as about resisting.

Those Anabaptist forefathers of mine would have counted Meyers as one of their own. To an idealistic young person, the Anabaptist vision was heady stuff. But having said that, I also realized that I was not, and have never been, an "out there on the edge" kind of guy. I like to stand back, hear from others first, then formulate my own thoughtful, careful response. A six-week stint as a human guinea pig at the National Institutes of Health (NIH) in Bethesda, Maryland, between my sophomore year at EMC and my junior year abroad experience in Japan, helped me "see myself" in this regard. It was the time of great protest and demonstration about the Vietnam War and other social and political issues, especially in the nation's capital. My roommate at NIH was out every day, participating in demonstrations. I was fascinated by his recounting of what seemed to me to be borderline illegal activities—a hunch that was confirmed when an FBI agent paid me a visit to ask about his activities. My roommate was sent home. While I was very sympathetic to the "causes" of the day, I was simply not wild and crazy about overtly exhibiting that sympathy. My style was to write a letter to the editor—and one such letter did get published in *The Washington Post*. While admiring them from afar, I doubt I would have been a good and faithful eighteenth-century Anabaptist.

Carol and Marriage

It was after returning from Japan and before starting my senior year at EMC that another event occurred that proved to be a solid mooring in my life for all the decades after. That was my marriage to Carol in 1971. We had met during spring break while both of us were first-year students at EMC. A male friend and I agreed to farm-sit for a local couple, enabling them to visit relatives out of state. Carol had elected to stay on campus and work during spring break rather than travel all the way back to Iowa for the short time off. My friend invited his friend—and two of her friends—to dinner one night. One of those two friends was Carol. I made Swiss steak, scalloped potatoes, and lima beans. My friend contributed the dessert after calling his mother for instructions. Between that initial meeting and our marriage, Carol spent a year in Holland through Mennonite Central Committee's International Volunteer Exchange Program, and I spent my junior year in Japan. I am sure Joseph Campbell, of whom I will write more following, would not present himself as a marriage counselor, but his words about marriage, slightly paraphrased, as quoted below from his book *An Open Life*, have rung true for me through the years.

> You see, the whole thing in marriage is the relationship and yielding—knowing the functions, knowing that each is playing a role in an organism. One of the things I have realized—and people who have been married a long

time realize—is that marriage is not just a love affair; it is much more. A love affair has to do with immediate personal satisfaction. But marriage is a challenge; it means yielding, time and again. That's why it's a sacrament; you give up your personal simplicity to participate in a relationship. And when you're giving, you're not giving to the other person: you're giving to the relationship. And if you realize that you are in the relationship just as the other person is, then it becomes life building, a life fostering and enriching experience, not an impoverishment because you're giving to somebody else.

The love affair with Carol has now surpassed forty-five years, more than twice the time I spent in my Dad's house. How did we begin our time together?

9

Washington, DC

The Guest House

AFTER GRADUATION FROM COLLEGE, Carol and I accepted a voluntary service assignment with the Mennonite Board of Missions as host and hostess of the International Guest House in Washington, DC. I also was attending American University studying international relations during that time. A voluntary service assignment for young adults, while not mandatory for Mennonites as for Mormons, was very common. It had its beginnings in the draft. With opposition to military service being a criterion for membership in the church, Mennonite young men had for years participated instead in alternate or voluntary service.

The Guest House was, and still is, a large older house located directly north of the White House just off 16th Street N.W. It had been converted to a small hostel for international visitors spending time in the nation's capital. The Allegheny Conference of the Mennonite Church, of which Hyattsville Mennonite Church in Hyattsville, Maryland, was a member, sponsored the House. While volunteering at the Guest House, we attended the Hyattsville Mennonite congregation, one of the most progressive in the Mennonite Church. Later the Hyattsville congregation was expelled from membership in the Conference over the issue of membership for homosexuals. For someone who was looking for a Mennonite Church that was not my father's church, to rephrase that old Oldsmobile car ad, this was as good as it got. It was a delightful group of folks with whom to associate.

On first thought, I might say my experiences at the Guest House proved more significant to my future professional life and career than to my spiritual life. I had taken no courses in business or management in college, but I began to realize I had some natural talent—and love for it. I also began to learn and appreciate the political skills needed to work successfully with a volunteer board of directors. The International Guest House operating board expressed great surprise and appreciation when I presented them with the first operations manual for the House. My operational and financial reports were timely, complete, and accurate—something they seemed not to have experienced prior. It was also my first foray into the quagmire of managerial ineptitude, in this case coupled with church politics. This learning by immersion experience was the catalyst for my beginning to formulate attitudes in my mind about ethical management practices and effective leadership. It began to form in my mind that the highest ethical or moral ground for any manager is attained when the interests of the "many" are successfully balanced vis-à-vis the few in pursuit of outcomes. You see, the whole point of management is to facilitate the "many" working toward a common goal. If you can then add leadership, which involves the "many" in coming to a consensus as to that shared goal, you have achieved the moral high ground. It was not until several years later that I discovered *The Servant Leader* and other writings by Robert K. Greenleaf. The leader as servant became my aspirational management and leadership style.

Carol and I, along with other staff, were volunteers. Volunteer staff members were either retired folks or young people who had not yet focused on family and career. Little did I know at the time, but it turned out to be a precursor to my eventual career work—relating to seniors, with a predominately young staff. In addition to volunteers, there was a paid director who had been the prime mover in founding the International Guest House years before. Unfortunately, as I was to re-learn many times thereafter, too often the person or group with the vision and hutzpah to start something is not the ideal person or people to continue operating it long term. We were told by a staff member of the Mennonite Board of Missions during orientation that the board of directors of the Guest House was becoming increasingly dissatisfied with their relationship with the paid director, but that would be an issue for the board and director, not Carol and my concern. Well, life doesn't work that way. At least, it didn't.

Upon arrival at the Guest House, it became immediately evident that the paid director had become a figure head at best, and often an obstacle to effective and efficient operations. Rather than assist, he hindered the volunteer staff in their day-to-day work and in accomplishing the mission of the House. The board was delighted to have someone on premises who was willing and able to confirm their long-standing suspicions. However, there was this overarching panoply of the paid director's relationship with the larger church and with ministers in that church. Let's just say, things got tense for a time. The usual cloud of righteous platitudes surfaced. My consistent position, along with other staff, was that on balance the director was detrimental to the work of the House, and it had proven impossible to be in conversation with him about any failings on his part. He was terminated. Carol and I became co-directors of the House.

The experiences at the Guest House affirmed for me that management and leadership provided the opportunity to accomplish so much more in life than one could ever do alone. A person working alone could never match the outcome of the many, well managed and led, toward a common goal. I found great joy and satisfaction in that work, even a sense of spiritual fulfillment. So yes, that time at the International Guest House was significant to my spiritual journey as well as to my professional journey. At the same time, I began to see and experience up close and personal what being involved in church leadership could entail. Did I want to go deeper into that well? Ready or not, there I went.

Hyattsville Mennonite Church

Our time at the Guest House was coming to an end. I was still working on a Master's Degree in International Relations at American University. The Hyattsville Mennonite congregation, in Hyattsville, Maryland, we had been attending was looking for pastoral leadership. The interim person was leaving, and the request was made that Carol take on the clerical work and that I assume a pastoral role with the congregation. I had great reservations about it, in particular about being a "pastor." We came up with two contingencies. First, the title for my role had to be congregational enabler, not interim pastor. Second, the vote by the congregation had to be unanimous. That second requirement was certainly not reflective of any mature sense of how the world works, but it was perhaps my way of putting out the fleece, hoping it would be dry come morning. Carol and I stood outside while the congregation voted. Someone came out and reported that both of our requirements were met. We moved into the church parsonage in University Park, Maryland.

Once again I thrived on the functionality of being the person "enabling" the work of the congregation, whether that was the Worship Task Force or other aspects of congregational life. The techniques of management and leadership are universal to any setting. I was also expected to speak from the pulpit two times a month. Those "sermons" became significant opportunities for more serious study and contemplation on religion and theology. I suspect the amount of reading and study I did would have matched any seminary level study and reading requirements. In addition, writing the sermons, along with several other articles, provided continued expression of "voice" during this time.

From the perspective of reinforcing traditional beliefs in my psyche, one of the most counter-productive activities I led during that time was a study series on church dogma and doctrine. It was a sweeping review of all the Christian Church universal had developed and held dear over the centuries. I remember thinking when planning the series that before I parted company with any of this baggage, I wanted to know and understand it. I am not sure what participants gained from the sessions; it left me with the un-mistakable self-awareness that my Christianity was not the Chris-tianity of majority Christians over time. It further reinforced my growing inclination to minimize belief and dogma and doctrine as the essence of Christianity and to emphasize personal ethics and behavior within the larger group. The gathering of the church was sacred, not because all members adhered to a set array of beliefs and dogma, but because they valued each other as persons; recog-nizing all as being on their own journey toward wholeness—rein-forced by taking care of each other, listening to one another, and enabling each other's true personhood. Such a church gathering is far more likely to encourage participants to reveal the radiance of their own discovery rather than to attempt to talk others into correct belief, a good thing from my perspective.

During my tenure as a congregational enabler, I wrote two additional articles. "What Should I Preach About Next Sunday?" was published in the June 1977 edition of *The Builder*, a publi-cation of the Mennonite Publishing House. The article suggested using a church calendar year concept for sermon topics to ensure full coverage of the Bible over the year. I adapted Paul Peachey's concept for the article. The idea of Sunday services and sermons following a church calendar year was usual and customary in many mainline Protestant churches, but it was certainly not part of Mennonite tradition and history. An article entitled "A Story About Congregational Involvement" was published in the June 8, 1976, edition of *Gospel Herald*. This publication was the story of the Hyattsville congregation finding itself without pastoral leader-ship and learning to function without it for several years, and then returning to traditional leadership.

After two periods of interim leadership, the Hyattsville con-gregation was ready to return to more traditional leadership. On my part, the experiences of self-directed theological education and the sharing of insights through sermons and in writing were very constructive. In addition to moving with greater intent away from dogma and belief, I also became increasingly definite that the traditional pastoral role was not for me long-term, even in a very progressive congregation. I have notes written while at Hyattsville expressing great personal angst about being seen as a visible leader in the church. I realized the more others saw me in that way, the more I reacted and wanted to move to the fringes of the church. I did not want to be accountable for this thing called "church" because of my misgivings about so much that went by that name.

I did come away from the Hyattsville experience with a life-long respect and appreciation for all the "pastoral counseling" demands on any pastor's life. I had no idea how being in that role opened one to the intimate and often ugly, complicated details of members' lives. One incident, with no participants still living, involved the death of the only son of a couple who were members. He was shot while attempting to enter a neighbor's house. No conclusion could be reached about whether he was drunk and disoriented, or breaking and entering. I was not prepared to be the counselor they deserved. I was happy to turn the Hyattsville congregation back to a newly arrived pastor and move on to other things.

Stereotypically, some may see the Midwest as flat and unexciting. Coming from the mountains and valleys of the Shenandoah Valley of Virginia, you may assume I'd be disenchanted with the Iowa landscape. Such was not the case. I found character and beauty in the landscape, and good people. And it was Carol's home.

10

Iowa

First Mennonite Church of Iowa City

Completing our work in Hyattsville Mennonite Church came just as a crisis struck in Carol's family, so the timing was fortuitous. Soon after leaving the leadership role at the Hyattsville congregation, Carol's mother received a diagnosis of cancer. Carol, the youngest daughter, felt compelled to return home to Iowa to be supportive of her mother and father. We had often talked of relocating to Iowa when raising a family became a priority for us, but this was making a decision in crisis mode. It turned out fine, though. After a short interim job in Iowa, three gentlemen came to visit me one Saturday evening. They introduced themselves as the officers of the board of directors of the local retirement community. Their mission was to ask if I would consider becoming administrator of that community. I told them I had come to enjoy management and business, but I knew nothing of retirement communities, that I had never even been in one. Actually, upon reflection, I remembered I had once gone to the door of the retirement community in Harrisonburg, Virginia, to hand a package to my sister who worked there. Still, I told them I would consider it.

My research quickly revealed that I would need a state-issued license to hold the administrator position, and to get that license I would have to get an AA degree in long-term care administration from Des Moines Area Community College in Ankeny, Iowa. The state of Iowa, at the time, accepted no other pathway to licensure. I told the board that it would take me about nine months to complete those degree requirements. They said they would pay for my education and hire a licensed administrator to be in the facility to meet state requirements throughout that time if I would accept the position and start as interim administrator. They did, and I did—and that is how I found my life-long career.

As soon as we relocated to Iowa, we began attending the First Mennonite Church in Iowa City. Some decisions turn out so much better than one could ever hope. The decision to participate with this congregation was one such decision. Not only could I be involved without the demands of official church leadership, but I also found a very congenial and welcoming Sunday school class, namely The Remnant class. As the name implies, the participants felt themselves somewhat as the remnant, not fitting in anywhere else. We became a solid group wherein non-traditional perspectives were given time and consideration without condemnation. Carol and I had moved from one progressive Mennonite congregation to another, and within that congregation, I found another life enriching small group. Needless to say, my idea of the true core and value of church life being the comradery of "fellow seekers on a journey" was further reinforced.

I did speak from the pulpit on several occasions while attending the Iowa City church. In one sermon I tried carefully to share of my spiritual journey without being too disruptive to the traditionalists in the audience. I gently questioned some of the church's dogma and suggested we'd been given minds to figure things out for our own time rather than blindly accepting the conclusions others had come to in centuries past. A Youth for Christ staff member in the audience was visually discombobulated. The instant the service concluded he was on the front platform, from his back pew, in my face, demanding, "Did I mean to suggest that all the New Testament writings about Jesus and his life and death may not have been actual verifiable historical facts?" If, by chance, you as the reader are not comfortable knowing my responses to these questions, perhaps this would be a good time to lay this book aside.

While the excessive commercialization of Christmas was never one of the most controversial issues facing the Mennonite Church or me personally, it did provide an interesting Iowa City church anecdote. After attending *The Twelve Days of Christmas* program at the Kennedy Center in Washington, DC, I wrote an article entitled "Commercialism and Christmas—Why Not?" The article was published in *Gospel Herald*. Wilbur Nachtigall, the congregation's pastor during part of our tenure, was preaching one Sunday. I was in that half-awake/half-asleep state of consciousness when suddenly my ears alerted my brain that the words from the pulpit were my own, as written sometime prior. I startled to full consciousness to hear Wilbur say, "These words are from an article written by Bernie Bowman."

Moving Anti-Homosexuality Thoughts Aside

While most Mennonite churches held societal and cultural issues at bay longer than other churches, still, in time, those same pressures came to bear on the Mennonite church. One that came to the church after my childhood was homosexuality. My understandings about homosexuality proved to be yet another example of how my world was expanding.

While homosexuality as an unsettled issue began percolating in my mind in college, it rose to serious consideration after college while living in the Washington, DC area. I grew up knowing nothing about homosexuality, except that it was a sin. Even when an older male began hanging out with my brother and me as young teenagers, I did not figure out on my own what it was about. When word spread that this young man "had issues," my Dad put a quick end to his coming over. But then as an adult I became acquainted with folks who were gay—and they seemed so normal. Or perhaps more accurately, I found out that folks I'd known for some time had been gay all along. Suddenly casting them as sinners just didn't compute in my brain. I cannot recall the book's title or the author's name, but reading the personal account of the mother of a gay son, a family of Mennonites, pushed me to the edge of complete acceptance. It was a chance happening at a bagel café in Iowa City that sealed the deal for me. I wrote a short piece after that encounter, but never submitted it for publication anywhere. The piece, entitled "Growing Up," appears in print here for the first time.

It was a treat to myself, Sunday morning breakfast at Brueggers while Carol joined choir practice. Just me, a pumpernickel bagel with olive and pimento cream cheese spread, a steaming mug of coffee, the Sunday paper, and an opportunity for people watching. Through the window, I noticed the arrival of a blue Camry. A blonde, in her late twenties, with straight hair that cambered in at the base of her neck and just over her ears, stepped out at the driver's side of the car. She was well-proportioned, handsome, and about five feet nine inches tall. Her companion was an inch or two shorter, about the same age, equally well-proportioned and cute, with long curly brown hair, the curls falling across her forehead and bouncing on her shoulders. I went back to reading my paper.

When next they caught my attention, they were headed toward a table directly in front of mine. The blonde clasped a Sunday paper under her left arm. She dropped the paper and moved the table closer to the window. Without a word, they sidled past each other so the brunette could sit with a view to the outside, the blonde facing me and the wall behind me. Their eyes met with winsome smiles as they sat down. More than friends, I mused. These people know each other very well—roommates perhaps?

The blonde thumbed through the sections of the newspaper, pulled out the Home and Real Estate section and began reading. The brunette split a bagel into halves and spread cream cheese on the top half before laying it on a napkin in front of the blonde. She put the bottom half, with no spread, on her side of the tray. The blonde was reading. The brunette gazed out the window, occasionally making comments to which the blonde responded—sometimes looking up from her paper, sometimes not.

Then I noticed their clothes. Both were dressed in light colored Docker-style slacks. The blonde wore a blue denim shirt, the brunette a blue pull-over sweater. They wore matching hiking boots. They looked like they belonged together, like long-married couples are prone to.

After a moment of comfortable silence, the brunette's face became animated. She reached across the table and clasped the fingers of the blonde, who lowered the paper, extended her hand, and squeezed her companion's hand. As the brunette began speaking, the blonde's eyes caressed her face.

I steadied the Life and Leisure section of the paper in front of my face, but the copy was not making the saltation from eye to brain. A smudge formed on the thumb of my left hand as a bead of sweat softened the ink. I fidgeted in the chair trying to avoid the amorous view directly in front of me. And just moments before the morning had seemed so perfect!

Resenting their intrusion into my comfortable world, I started to fold my paper. But I hesitated. My eye caught the title of a book review in the paper—*Growing Up* by Russell Baker. Growing up!?

My mind left the present and drifted back to a day in early March years ago. It was as if a death had occurred in my family, the death of a maxim my parents and their parents before them held dear. No one in my family married a Catholic. It jeopardized one's chances for passage through the pearly gates, and it ruined the family name. But my brother was not to be dissuaded. I remembered the angry outbursts juxtaposed with hushed, somber tones. I remembered aunts and uncles commiserating as though at a wake. My Father sulked his clear intent to have nothing to do with his next to oldest son and his new daughter-in-law.

My parents relented and attended the wedding, as did I. Other than their proclivity to stand, sit, and kneel in rapid succession in the service, and the presence of alcoholic beverages at the reception, the bride's people seemed a lot like my people.

I grew up and moved away. My brother raised a family in the same town as my parents. Now, years later when I call home to see how my aging parents are faring, the conversation with them often includes comments such as, "Your brother was just here and took care of this or that," and, "We don't know what we'd do without him and his wife."

Back at Brueggers, the couple was just leaving. I noticed their clasped fingers and their faces turned toward each other. I smiled. It was a perfect morning.

Further Education

Having decided that retirement community administration was to be my career, at least for the foreseeable future, I realized that previous education aside, if I wanted not to be denied opportunity in my chosen career field, I needed a related master's degree. The University of Iowa in Iowa City had a renowned program in hospital and healthcare administration. I met with the head of the department, asking how I might balance graduate study with full-time work, plus maintaining some semblance of family life. His response was "in my face" unmistakable. He had no interest in flexing their program around anyone. His interest was in recent college graduates who could and would focus all their energies on study. I told the department head at the University of Iowa that in the future he would be recruiting folks like me for their program. In the meantime, I would take my money and my aspirations to the University of Minnesota. Before visiting the University of Iowa, I had done enough research to know the University of Minnesota had a program established exclusively for practicing administrators. Anyone aspiring to acceptance in the Minnesota program had to have at least five years of practical work experience. Minnesota proved to be the greatest educational experience of my life. There is nothing like education with and among others, all with the maturity that a bit of age and work experience brings.

Several years later, I received the Master's Degree in Hospital and Health Care Administration. In addition to the pleasure and satisfaction I received from acquiring the Master's Degree, it also proved very helpful in future job searches, as I had anticipated.

11

Influence of Joseph Campbell, Science Writers, the Jesus Seminar, and Jung

Reading

READING HAS ALWAYS BEEN my go-to activity. My fifth-grade classroom at Mt. Clinton Elementary School had a small library at the back of the room; I suspect it was a collection of the teacher's personal books. The teacher issued a challenge to the class, offering a prize to the student who read the most books during the year. I read eighty-five books during the school year and won the prize. Toward the end of the year, the teacher would ask me questions about each book as I returned it, no doubt testing to see if I was reading. I learned later in life that I strongly preferred sensory input that is visual, perhaps related to a love of reading. Incidentally, an equally important learning for me was that my weakest sensory input is auditory. Staff would often use the opportunity when walking with me in and around a building or a retirement community campus to tell me something they deemed important. I learned to both pause and write myself a note, often on my hand, or if a longer reminder was necessary, to tell them to put their words in writing to me if they wanted to be sure I "heard" them.

I spent a lot of time reading books and material related to the two additional degrees related to my profession, but that did not keep me from reading for personal entertainment and growth. From the fiction world, I thoroughly enjoyed all of Jean Auel's novels, starting with the *Clan of the Cave Bear* set in prehistoric times, and most of James Michener's time-sweep novels. From the world of British comedy, to my appraisal it doesn't get much better than John Mortimer's Rumpole series. At the suggestion of a friend, I read, and thoroughly enjoyed, Louis L'amour's western genre books.

But it was the non-fiction world of books that most influenced my odyssey. Initially, it was back and forth between books about myth, especially Joseph Campbell's work, and physics books about the cosmos. Later it was publications from the emerging Jesus Seminar movement, along with books by and about Carl Jung, that moved me toward a greater understanding of myself and my place in the world. As a series of paintings over time represent the "evolvement" of the artist, so the books annotated below represent milestones in my awakening. To see the picture that evolved, read on. Where it seems important, I have given page numbers from the editions of the books cited. A bibliography also is included in the last pages of this book, should the reader want to read more.

Joseph Campbell and The World's Other Religions

My first exposure to Joseph Campbell was his book *The Hero with a Thousand Faces*. I came to know and understand, for the first time, those overarching truths at the core of spiritual and psychological belief systems of all cultures and in all times and all places. Wow! I was fascinated to learn of parallel myths across different cultures and historical eras. I admit, when initially exposed to the world's myths, my inclination was to understand all others as fantasy, while clinging to an understanding of traditional

Christian myths as fact. But as I came to understand that all myths are the same, in that they represent humankind's efforts at finding our place in this world, then my own—both my own traditional Christian myths and those I came to adopt from others—came to have greater spiritual and interpretative value. I developed empathy with Campbell when he asserted that contemporary culture, in particular Western culture, had moved progressively away from self-understanding and self-awareness that can be found in myths—to their detriment.

Campbell's book *The Flight of the Wild Gander,* especially its conclusion on page 225, provided me with hours of contemplative thought. I quote the first part of that conclusion here—and invite you to reflect and think about it with me.

> For it is simply an incontrovertible fact that, with the rise of modern science, the entire cosmological structure of the Bible and the church has been destroyed and not the cosmological only but the historical as well. The gradual, irresistible, steady development of this new realization of the wonder of the world and of man's place and possibilities within it, against every instrument of resistance of the Church—resistance even to the present hour—has been, and continues to be, the fruit of the labors of a remarkably small number of men with wit and courage to oppose authority with accurate observation.

The more I read and learned of man's quest for understanding of our place here on earth, over eons of time and around the globe, the less I could accept as workable any religion or spiritual ethos that set itself apart and above all others. There is no doubt in my mind; each person must search and find what works for them. We are all different, so it is not surprising that what works for one will not satisfy another. I don't have a problem with anyone feeling strong that their particular religious or spiritual expression is the only one for them; even being excited about sharing their beliefs with others. It is when someone presents a given expression as the only true expression that I turn away.

Becoming aware of the Dalai Lama's famous quote, "The purpose of our lives is to be happy," is just one example of how my world expanded. Lest you think the Dalai Lama is shallow or that his admonition is simple and easy, be sure to put these words in the context of his life of resistance and nurture of others—and of people's efforts over the eons to find true happiness. Finding what brings true happiness is one of the greatest of life's challenges. In the end, it is usually a great paradox, just the opposite of what we first imagine. It takes most of us a lifetime of living to even begin to figure out what truly makes us happy. After all, the pinnacle of wisdom and maturity is the ability to hold paradox comfortably within oneself—and what makes for happiness is usually a great paradox.

As regards the various "isms" relating to philosophy and religion, I do find some empathy with panentheism (as distinct from pantheism). Definitions vary, but I relate to a definition of panentheism as an understanding that some cosmic animating force interpenetrates every other part of the universe and perhaps extends beyond it. Whatever that cosmic animating force before or behind the Big Bang, it remains with and within us; we are one with all that is. But, again, I feel no need to attempt to prove or disprove, to convince or to persuade.

Science, Physics, and Cosmology

There can be no better introduction to musings about science than a quote from Charles Darwin from the introduction to *The Descent of Man*. It is as follows:

> It has often and confidently been asserted, that man's origin can never be known: but ignorance more frequently begets confidence than does knowledge: it is those who know little, and not those who know much, who so positively assert that this or that problem will never be solved by science.

For most of human history, people turned to religion for answers to basic questions of human existence. How did the universe and our earth begin? How did life begin—and from whence came humans—and for what purpose? In my early growing up years, I did not question the Christian church's answers to these questions. But it is hard to attend school and to begin to think with any independence without coming to realize that science in the last several hundred years has begun providing answers to these same questions. And the answers from science are credible, based on solid evidence, sometimes at odds with the traditional answers from religion. What follows is an eclectic sampling of books I read in science, physics, and cosmology early in my odyssey.

One of my least favorite courses in college was physics. I did OK grade-wise, but I truly just memorized the facts so as to regurgitate them on test day. Later I found reading physics books about the cosmos to be such a delight, causing me to reflect back on college physics. Was it the teacher or perhaps my stage of life at the time? Then it dawned on me; it was the difference between theoretical versus experimental physics. It was the work of theoretical physicists that so captured my interest and imagination.

Paul Davies, in his book *God and the New Physics,* lays out the claims of traditional religion against the findings of science (or new physics) as they relate to the questions above, inviting the reader to ponder seeming contradictions. As he says, in many cases it is not that science has disproven religion; rather, science has simply transcended religion. Granted, some may read Davies as a full out attack on religion; I did not see it as such, and most appreciated his balance as to what can be learned from science. He talks about a juxtaposition of reductionism and holism. Western scientific inquiry—both physics and biology—has been solely reductionist in the last centuries. The question is not which is correct; rather which should be used, depending on what you want to know. To quote Davies from page 62:

> In the case of living systems, nobody would deny that an organism is a collection of atoms. The mistake is to suppose that it is nothing but a collection of atoms. Such a claim is as ridiculous as asserting that a Beethoven symphony is nothing but a collection of notes or that a

> Dickens novel is nothing but a collection of words. The property of life, the theme of a tune, or the plot of a novel are what have been called 'emergent' qualities. They only emerge at the collective level of structure and are simply meaningless at the component level. The component description does not contradict the holistic description; the two points of view are complimentary, each valid at their own level.

We may or may not agree with Davies's beginning and ending assertion that "science offers a surer path than religion in the search of God." For someone like me who had only heard the traditional Christian assertion on this, Davies's quote required me to stretch my mind. It is very hard to argue with another Davies' assertion on page 229, "The new physics has overturned so many commonsense notions of space, time and matter that no serious religious thinker can ignore it." Not only did I find I could not ignore it, but it was absolutely mind-blowing new information.

Those who have not studied evolution, or who are ideologically disposed to disbelieve in evolution, usually have an immediate gut reaction to the concept of man having evolved from apes. The evidence for man evolving from other species, including the ape, is so overwhelming; it is hard for me to remember a time when that idea troubled so many. How much more sacred and exciting it is for me to contemplate life beginning those eons ago in the sea, with evolutionary processes bringing that life to fruition in me today, than to merely assert that God created an earlier version of me, full blown in the Garden. While the specific aquatic theory Elaine Morgan espouses in her book *The Aquatic Ape* has not gained a large following, the book itself is a delightful and easy to read primer on the theory of human evolution. Many other books trace our evolution as humans, but Morgan's book is a good recommended first read.

Reading *The Universe Story: A Celebration of the Unfolding of the Cosmos,* by Brian Swimme and Thomas Berry, was a transformational experience for me. Their work brings together the celebratory story of earth and the universe as seen through our observational sciences, inclusive of the human dimension. As they say in the introduction on page 5, "Every living being on earth is cousin to every other living being. Even beyond the realm of the living we have a common origin in the primordial Flaring Forth of the energies from which the universe in all its aspects is derived." The authors tell a convincing story of the universe on page 3 as a celebration of existence and life and consciousness; of the earth seeming to be a "reality that is developing with the simple aim of celebrating the joy of existence." But juxtaposed to this celebratory story is another story on pages 254 and 255.

> That our western civilization should be the principal cause of such extensive damage to the planet is so difficult a truth for us to absorb that our society, in general, is presently in a state of shock and denial, of disbelief that such can possibly be the real situation. We are unable to move from a conviction that as humans we are the glory and crown of the earth community to a realization that we are the most destructive and the most dangerous component of that community. . . . The crash that faces us is not the crash simply of the human, it's a crash of the bio-systems of the earth; indeed it is in some manner the crash of the earth itself.

Swimme and Berry's *The Universe Story: A Celebration of the Unfolding of the Cosmos*, along with many other inputs, convinces me that we need—we must get to—a religion that acknowledges our earth as sacred and our stewardship of it for future generations of far greater import than the narrow goal of figuring out how to escape from earth to heaven.

The book *God's Laughter: Physics, Religion and the Cosmos*, by Gerhard Staguhn, helped me understand that if one wants to look seriously for God, it must be done independently of ideology and dogma. Instead, one has to take into account what appears to us as two infinities on either side of our own existence; the infinity before and the infinity after. When we do that, we find, no doubt, commonality with Augustine of Hippo, the early church theologian, who concludes: "If you understand God, it is not God you understand." If God exists, he can only be where human knowledge cannot reach him. In Staguhn's conclusion, on page 254, he quotes Julian Huxley, the British evolutionary biologist

> Many people assert that this abandonment of the god hypothesis means the abandonment of all religion and all moral sanctions. This is simply not true. But it does mean . . . that we must construct something to take its place. Though gods and God in any meaningful sense seem destined to disappear, the stuff of divinity out of which they have grown and developed remains. A humanist evolution-centered religion also needs divinity, but . . . it must strip the divine of the theistic qualities which man has anthropomorphically projected into it . . . .

It was one of those "ah-ha" moments along the journey when I realized that if I had to choose between a God who was created in our own image, within the bounds of what we can know and describe and understand, or a God that is, by definition, beyond what we can know, describe, or fully understand, I would take the latter any time.

Staguhn's book *God's Laughter*, along with input from other resources, helped me come to a new understanding of death. I was exposed to the frequent occurrence of death, through my work, over many years. Still it never became routine. I came to understand that life is not sacred because it has a beginning. It is not the creation of life that makes it sacred; it is the death of all things living that makes the life we experience between birth and death sacred. Without an end to life, there would be nothing singular or extraordinary about our time alive. The imagery of "God knowing us before we were born" may be comforting and reassuring to our existence now that we've arrived, but, in reality, the beginning of all life is serendipitous. Think about the flight of the bee that deposits a speck of pollen here instead of there; or the wind that carries spores to one plant and not another. The beginning of human life is no different. We all began from some fortuitous union of a single sperm with an egg. Our parents could just as easily have never met, or a different sperm may have reached home base first.

But it happened! I was conceived and survived all the uncertainties of prenatal development. But what was the "self" that was birthed? As years progressed and my insights deepened, I became increasingly aware that my "self" did not stop with my body or mind and thoughts, even with my skin, my outer shell. What a thrill to realize that my "self" was and is "one" with the entire earth, with the universe, the cosmos. The stuff (atoms) of which I was made are just released at the natural end of my body and mind, becoming building blocks once again subject to cosmic disposal.

It is deeply comforting to me, knowing that my larger "self" lives on as part of the cosmos. For me, it has not been the hope of heaven or the fear of hell that motivated me to action during my life. I cannot prove or disprove that heaven or hell is real, nor do I feel any need to do so, but the answer to that question became non-consequential to my life. Once I acknowledged the mortality of my human self, it became apparent that I had but the briefest window of opportunity to live; only a fleeting flicker of time in which to delight in the sacred life I'd been given. It was the life I had in the here and now that mattered, not some fanciful life hereafter. The larger "self" that may live on most undoubtedly does not do so in any recognizable form, only as elements in some other manifestation of the cosmos.

An arms-length or perhaps universe-length perspective on our life and death might suggest that upon death we go to the same place we came from before we were conceived. What happens in the physical world is that bacteria consume our cells, and we return to dust. We've all heard this transition referred to as "coming from God and returning to God." Others prefer the imagery of "coming from mystery and returning to mystery." For me, the bookend imagery of "coming from the stars and returning to the stars" is a grand, beautiful, and deeply spiritual image. Just think. This form of flesh and mind, emotions and ideas, joys and sorrows, this reality of life—me—I came from the stars and I return to the stars. What could be more amazing! Nothing could be more sacred; sacred defined as highly valued and important, deserving of great respect and awe. In what feels to us like an infinite universe, I came to know and experience life for a moment, a life given meaning and purpose by its very finiteness. It is not so much that death gives meaning to life, but that death provides the other bookend to life. Without that other bookend, life would be nothing exceptional, nothing sacred.

Rumi's poetry, as translated by Coleman Barks, is just one example of people in other times and other cultures thinking about these things. I love his poem "Whoever Brought Me Here."

> All day I think about it, then at night I say it.
> Where did I come from, and what am I supposed to be doing?
> I have no idea.
> My soul is from elsewhere, I'm sure of that,
> and I intend to end up there.
> This drunkenness began in some other tavern.
> When I get back around to that place,
> I'll be completely sober. Meanwhile,
> I'm like a bird from another continent, sitting in this aviary.
> The day is coming when I fly off,
> but who is it now in my ear who hears my voice?
> Who says words with my mouth?
> Who looks out with my eyes? What is the soul?
> I cannot stop asking.
> If I could taste one sip of an answer
> I could break out of this prison for drunks.
> I didn't come here of my own accord, and I can't leave that way.
> Whoever brought me here, will have to take me home.

Moving to an example of a book about the wonder and majesty of our universe, its formation, and its current existence, I recommend Martin Rees's *Our Cosmic Habitat*. In the introduction, Rees suggests that while the preeminent mystery of why anything exists at all is the province of philosophers and theologians, "For science, the overarching problem is to understand how a genesis event so simple that it can be described by a short recipe seems to have led, thirteen billion years later, to the complex cosmos of which we are a part. Was the outcome 'natural,' or should we be surprised at what happened? Could there be other universes?" Rees's conclusion on page 181 is enough to keep a person thinking for decades. Does it get any more exciting than this?

> No mystery in cosmology presents a more daunting challenge than the task of fully elucidating how atoms assembled—here on earth and perhaps on other worlds—into living beings intricate enough to ponder their origins.

Perhaps the best book I've read relating specifically to the human experience provides answers to any number of questions. Would you like to know how apes slowly morphed into humans? Or to see a map of the route humans took out of Africa and their subsequent migrations? Would you like to know about the formation of social institutions as humankind transitioned from nomads to hunter-gatherers to complex societies? How about knowing when humans lost their body hair, and gained speech, or started to sew their clothes? The book *Before the Dawn,* by Nicholas Wade, provides a new and far more detailed picture of human evolution, human nature, and history—of all things—from the record that is encoded in the DNA of the human genome. Those who compiled the Bible, utilizing the myths and legends of their time, did their best to explain us humans. For example, they offered an explanation as to why people speak in different languages; why women suffer pain in childbirth; and why they wear clothes to hide their nakedness. Science, in particular DNA, is allowing us to re-write that history, to offer new understandings of origins, and transformations thereafter. It is a great, exciting time to be alive. To not use the new tools of inquiry we've developed toward writing and re-writing understandings for our time would be to betray our humanness.

Coming from a classic theistic God perspective, some may find it challenging to integrate their religion with science, but be unwilling to move as far as I have toward a non-theistic God. Two recent publications may be helpful in finding a way forward that, according to these authors, does not require the abandonment of a realist, theistic God. In his book *Darwin in a New Key*, William

Meyer, a professor at Maryville College in Maryville, Tennessee, applies process theology to Darwin and evolution in a way he feels not only allows but calls for a revised theistic God, one that is not at odds with Darwin's amazing insights. Another similar reference is Bryon Bangert's article in *The Fourth R, March-April 2016* edition, in which he argues that process theology has eliminated the need to abandon a realist, theistic conception of God.

I close this section by recounting a visit to the Creation Museum in Petersburg, Kentucky. I never intended to visit, but brother Eldon was insistent that we go. Eldon said he had one question he knew they could not answer. That is, "How did animals get to Australia?" If all the animals died in the flood and only those on the ark were left to repopulate the earth, how could they have gotten to Australia? Well, the Museum had a display dedicated to answering the question. Whenever a large flood occurs considerable flotsam is created. Given the size of this flood, exceedingly huge mats of trees and brush and other debris were formed, and upon these mats the animals from Noah's ark traveled from present-day Turkey to Australia. Now, apart from the sheer implausibility of animals getting on and floating thousands of miles on flotsam, the Bible does say that all the animals not on the ark perished. And the animals on the ark were not let out until the flood had receded and dry land re-appeared. Obviously, it would have taken years for the ark animals to multiply to the point where they could be shared with Australia, and long before that time those huge flotsam mats would no longer be floating around. But why let scientific fact impinge upon ideology? I have no issue with anyone who elects to believe the Genesis creation and Noah flood stories. That is their choice. The Noah flood story is a delightful legend, shared by hundreds of cultures across the globe. I do take serious umbrage with the creators of the Creation Museum presenting their ideas about creation and the flood as science. That is a tragedy and a lie because they know it is not science by any current definition of that term. I watched all the children coming to the Museum that day and could only hope that their life journeys will give them an opportunity to come to understand science as something other than what they saw and heard at the Creation Museum.

Jesus Seminar

As my understanding grew of how myth had been part of the human experience across the world and across eons, and as I came to appreciate what science had to tell us about our world and our place in it, I had to find a way to think about religion that worked. I had long since departed from the religion of my father, but dismissing it entirely did not seem a good option. The Jesus Seminar, a group of 150 scholars and laypersons founded in 1985 by Robert Funk, an American biblical scholar, under the auspices of the Westar Institute, proved to be that primary resource in finding a place of comfort with intellectual integrity. Incidentally, this Robert Funk was not related to the John Funk or Joseph Funk noted in the confusion associated with my college senior paper.

As is often the case, it was other people who pointed me in the direction of the Jesus Seminar. At about the point of my first awareness of The Jesus Seminar, my daughter, home from college, gave me a copy of Marcus Borg's book *Meeting Jesus Again for the First Time*, and a friend, an Episcopal priest and family counselor, gave me a copy of Borg's book *Jesus A New Vision*.

I found a religious perspective in the Jesus Seminar movement's publications that did not require me to leave my brain asunder when contemplating religious or spiritual matters. That Episcopal priest, along with a retired Baptist minister and yours truly, worked to bring the first Jesus Seminar presentation to Cedar Rapids, Iowa. The irony of a Mennonite layperson, a Baptist minister, and an Episcopal priest working together in this effort still brings a smile to my face. The rebuttal of some folks in the audience to one of the presentations only gave me greater confidence this was a way forward that worked for me. I knew my understanding of Christianity was not in sync with that of the person mounting the rebuttal.

A quote by Alan Jones, Dean of Grace Cathedral in San Francisco, in the front of Borg's *Meeting Jesus Again for the First Time* best summarizes the effect of this book on me. "Borg liberates 'Jesus' from the rigidity of fundamentalism and the aridity of intellectualism. He also graciously liberates readers from the shackles of what many have thought they were supposed to believe about Jesus if they were to remain Christians. What a relief to see Jesus in a totally new light."

Other meaningful quotes from the book are included on pages 3, 9, 13, 14, and 37, respectively:

- That life is ultimately not about believing or about being good. Rather, it is about a relationship with God that involves us in a journey of transformation.

- The gospels are neither divine documents nor straightforward historical records. They are not divine products inspired directly by God, whose contents therefore are to be believed. Nor are they eyewitness accounts written by people who had accompanied Jesus and simply sought to report what they had seen and heard. Rather, the gospels represent the developing traditions of the early Christian movement.

- Moreover, the longer I studied the Christian tradition, the more transparent its human origins became. Religions in general, it seemed to me, were manifestly cultural products. I could see how their readily identifiable psychological and social functions served human needs and cultural ends. The notion that we made it all up was somewhat alarming, but also increasingly compelling.

- Partially paraphrased: These *aha* moments gave me a new understanding of the meaning of the word *God*. I realized that *God* does not refer to a supernatural being "out there." Rather, I began to see, the word *God* refers to the sacred at the center of existence, the holy mystery that is all around us and within us.

- The image I have sketched views Jesus differently: rather than being the exclusive revelation of God, he is one of many mediators of the sacred.

Some meaningful quotes from *Jesus A New Vision* are included on pages 7–8, 70, and 142 respectively:

- In short, the image of the historical Jesus as a divine or semi-divine being, who saw himself as the divine savior whose purpose was to die for the sins of the world, and whose message consisted of proclaiming that, is simply not historically true. Rather it is the product of a blend produced by the early church.

- In their historical context, the miracles of Jesus do not "prove" that he was divine. In the tradition in which he stood, including figures from its ancient past and persons contemporary with him, the healings and exorcisms reported of him were not unique.

- Historically speaking, Jesus sought to transform his social world by creating an alternative community structured around compassion, with norms that moved in the direction of inclusiveness, acceptance, love and peace.

What truly is Christianity? I appreciate Lloyd Geering's thinking on this as expressed in an article entitled "Christianity Faces the New Millennium" in the Jesus Seminar journal *The Fourth R*, January/February 1999 edition. It helps if we recognize that all theology is a human construct. If we take our human constructions too seriously, we become idolaters. The most heinous sin in the eyes of the biblical writers was not atheism, but idolatry. So what actually is Christianity, as enumerated by Geering in his article?

- Is it "the faith which was once for all delivered to the saints" as stated in Jude 3?

- Is it the belief system expressed in the creeds and confessions of the church—including the doctrine of the Trinity, virgin birth and incarnation, and others?

- Does Christianity consist of living a sacramental life within the authoritative institutional structures called Mother Church?

- Is the essence of Christianity found in accepting Jesus Christ as one's personal Lord and Savior?

- Does Christianity mean accepting uncritically a set of ancient Scriptures as the written record of what is ultimately true?

- Does Christianity consist simply of a set of moral values by which to live?

Various "Christian" sects or groups have embraced one or more of these definitions over time as the essence of Christianity. Furthermore, from modern research, we know there was never a time when all Christians shared the same beliefs or understandings of what it meant to be a Christian. It has changed, it is changing, and it will change going forward.

I love Geering's image of Christianity and share it with you here, " . . . as a stream of living culture flowing through the plains of time as a river." As it flows, it divides into sub-streams. It joins other streams. At times, it gathers new material from the bank as it passes. Some times that material crystalizes into solid objects. Other times material drops out as sediment. People tend to look at things like the ministry or priesthood, church governance, creeds and dogmas, and the Bible itself as the essence of the stream. It may be difficult to accept at first hearing, but, in fact, these visible elements have less permanence than the stream which carries them along.

As Geering reminds us, critics of reform have always said reformers are throwing the baby out with the bath water. In fact, there is no permanent or absolute essence of Christianity. There is no baby—only bath water—which is the ongoing cultural stream of Judeo-Christian traditions.

From all these readings, I came to realize that religion of all sorts is a human construct. What we have today was passed on to us from prior human activity. It is not sacreligious, nor arrogant, for us to step up in our time to construct a religion that works for us in our time. Who knows, if we tend that sacred duty with great care and thought, we may produce something to offer future generations—for their eventual acceptance or renovation.

I have since read many, many books by Jesus Seminar Fellows, but a couple of especially significant others early on in my odyssey included: *A History of God* by Karen Armstrong; *Who Wrote the New Testament?* by Burton Mack; *Honest to Jesus* by Robert W. Funk; and A *New Christianity for a New World* by John Shelby Spong. Karen Armstrong concludes her book A *History of God* on page 399 as follows:

> Human beings cannot endure emptiness and desolation; they will fill the vacuum by creating a new focus of meaning. The idols of fundamentalism are not good substitutes for God; if we are to create a vibrant new faith for the twenty-first century, we should, perhaps, ponder the history of God for some lessons and warnings.

Jung

I learned in being married to Carol that I did not begin adult life with a great intuitive sense of my inner world or anyone else. But the thought and work of Carl Jung helped immensely in moving me along that continuum toward greater sensitivity. After all, as Jung posits, a life lived successfully is one long movement toward wholeness, toward completion. While I read Jung's writings, it was helpful to read others' writings about Jung's work. For example, *Jung: A Beginner's Guide* by Ruth Berry and *Jung's Analytical Psychology and Religion* by Carl Alfred Meier, MD. One in particular who utilized Jung's work in a way that spoke to me was Robert A. Johnson and his books *HE* and *SHE*. I came to understand far more about masculine psychology from Parsifal's search for the Holy Grail, as expounded upon by Johnson in *HE* than I had ever learned in Sunday school or from reading the Holy Scriptures.

Jerry Ruhl, who wrote Johnson's life story in *Balancing Heaven and Earth*, says Johnson's life is a remarkable example of how to live with a religious attitude in postmodern times. Ruhl explains, "By religious attitude, I am not referring to following in a path toward redemption or salvation or to being a member of a religious institution. A religious attitude refers to the cultivation of soul—an openness to wonder, awe and reverence with respect to . . . those numinous forces that exist outside our conscious control." I found great empathy with Jung's assessment that dogmatic fundamentalist religions tended to be unhelpful; that religions need to grow and evolve to answer the deep spiritual needs of ordinary people. Or to put it in my words, I believe many different frameworks can be useful in a person's journey into wholeness. Yes, the traditional Christian Church can be a useful crucible for the journey, but my bias suggests that many who want to travel long distances on the journey find the traditional church, with all its trappings, to be less than helpful, if not suffocating. I certainly did.

As one example of how I found Jung's concepts helpful, consider the classic Christian doctrine of original sin. There is a dark side in all of humanity. There is also, in all religious traditions, the possibility of a reversal from walking a path that is harmful to oneself and others to a better and more productive path. For me, Jung's concept of "shadow" is a far more helpful way to think about the dark side than original sin. Robert A. Johnson's book *Owning Your Own Shadow: Understanding the Dark Side of the Psyche* proved especially helpful.

While not strictly a book about Jung, *Iron John*, by Robert Bly, proved significant to my odyssey. Someone has described the book as a delightful meditation on the application of folklore, archetype, psychology, and history to an enriched sense of manhood. I found it so. Reading the book *Iron John* also made me aware that I had unconsciously adopted a pattern of finding mentors in board chairs associated with my work. No doubt I was searching for that style of mentoring I had not found in my father.

12

Maryville, Tennessee

I CONFESS TO A bit of pride that at the three CEO positions I held, at the time I left, I had served longer than any previous holder of the position. However, I have always been of the opinion that both the organization and its leader are well served if they do not remain attached for life. I have no idea of the ideal tenure before moving on, but I always wanted to move on before others thought it was time. In 1998, after fourteen and a half years working in Cedar Rapids, Iowa, and before that, seven and a half years working in Kalona, Iowa, we relocated to Maryville, Tennessee, where I had accepted a new CEO position. Fortunately, we found another Sunday school group in a United Methodist Church with many of the characteristics of the group we left in Iowa.

Given my position as CEO in an organization affiliated with the United Methodist Church, I was invited, at times, to participate in Holston Conference activities. At one of those politically correct banquets, I was seated next to a soon-to-be-retiring United Methodist minister. Without any prodding from me, he volunteered that he could hardly wait to talk openly about his discovery that he had become a Christian agnostic. I found myself in sympathy both to his circumstance and to his self-label. As he said, "I cannot erase having been Christian, but now I have more questions than answers." As the conversation turned to the question of meaning or purpose in life, we found a common acknowledgment that life itself, as portrayed by a strict Darwinian interpretation, is simply protoplasm with the urge to reproduce. However, it is each distinct incarnation of life that has potentiality; hence the purpose of life—or as one might say the highest experience of life—is to live that potentiality.

After two years, in that great tradition of Methodism, there was a transition in pastoral leadership at the United Methodist Church we attended—a transition that made it challenging for us to continue with Sunday morning services there. We found ourselves more at home in one of the local Presbyterian churches, where, again, a Sunday school class proved to be a welcoming and open minded group of seekers.

Maryville provided fresh opportunity for writing, something I had not made a priority in the last years in Iowa.

13

Gilgamesh's Answer

As you've recognized, I have cherry picked from many sources and resources along my odyssey in coming to my own answers to life's great questions—Where did we come from? Why are we here? Where are we going? What is our purpose while here? Or, as the question formed in my mind over time, "What experiences in living provide that sense of being at one with all else?" Perhaps it is evident to the reader, but still it is important for me to acknowledge that I am not, and have never been, an original thinker in life. I realize this is factual to some extent for everyone. One of the most interesting things I read about Albert Einstein was a book about the books that Einstein read during his school years before he developed his theories. We all, even Einstein, build on the shoulders of those who came before us. Still, I am far better at taking the work of others, whether in my professional or my personal life, and re-forming it to my needs than I have been in creating something entirely new.

In that vein of thinking, if I had to select a single hero to emulate in finding answers to these great questions of life it would be Gilgamesh. His answers are intellectually honest, brave, and to me, very comforting and satisfying. Perhaps you are not acquainted with Gilgamesh, so let me recount his story, but first an introduction.

As noted, East Tennessee became our place of residence in 1998. Soon after that, I had the good fortune to be invited to join The Thinkers Group, a gathering of twelve men. To this day, the group meets monthly in members' homes. At each meeting, a member presents a paper, followed by questions and discussion. For my first paper, I decided to share the story of Gilgamesh. It was my way of sharing by extrapolation my world and religious views as they had developed up to that time. I was, and am, deeply indebted to Robert A. Oden Jr., who told the story of Gilgamesh in a lecture available from The Teaching Company's Great Courses. What follows is an edited and abbreviated version of the Thinkers Group paper I presented in 2003.

> My paper this evening will reflect my thinking as it has evolved over time. Since the dawn of human consciousness, people have been probing the "what makes life worth living" questions. How do we understand and make sense of this human condition? Why are we here? What sets us apart, as humans, from say, animals or gods? The epic of Gilgamesh provides an answer; perhaps one that will surprise you. I believe Gilgamesh's answer is as instructional today as it was when first inscribed in Mesopotamia around 2,500 BCE. The epic, just like the Christian Bible, is a compilation of writings from many sources over many years, all redacted into a coherent story.
>
> As for the story itself, Gilgamesh is a remarkable young man, probably sixteen to eighteen years of age at the opening of the epic. He is one-third human and two-thirds divine. We may smile at that idea of shared humanity and divinity. Some may immediately dismiss the story for that fact alone. But, tell me, how is that different from another religious figure whom we, as Christians, consider both fully human and fully divine?
>
> To continue the epic, Gilgamesh is King of the city of Uruk at that tender age. When I introduced Gilgamesh as remarkable, I mean truly incredible. He is

unsurpassed at everything. He is the smartest, the fastest, the strongest, and the finest at everything. He is so gifted that he exhausts his subjects. They cannot keep pace with him. Gilgamesh is even able to seduce all the young "brides to be" before their wedding nights. You can see why his people had just had it with him. But the Mesopotamian solution was not to kill him. Oh, no, that would have deprived society of Gilgamesh's great assets.

The people find a better solution. They search for a double for him, someone who can keep up, be his match, so they do not have to be exposed to all his energy and stamina. Enkidu is found, out in the field, running wild with the beasts. He has all the physical and mental attributes to be a match for Gilgamesh. But they have to tame him down, get the country out of him. He has to become urbanized if he is to dwell in the town of Uruk with Gilgamesh.

How do you take the country out of someone? The town's citizens negotiate with a prostitute, asking her to go out to the fields and seduce Enkidu. Enkidu and the prostitute spend seven wonderful nights together—after which Enkidu discovers he cannot go back to his old life. Enkidu has been "to town" and there is no going back. His former companions, the beasts of the field, will not take him back.

The people take Enkidu to town where he meets Gilgamesh. The two of them have the mother of all fights; neither can triumph, so finally they give up and become best buddies. Gilgamesh and Enkidu go on a series of exploits together, having a great time matching each other with prowess and skill. The people love having Gilgamesh otherwise engaged.

But then Enkidu dies!

Gilgamesh is devastated. He has to face the human condition. Death and mortality have stared him in the face. How can he respond? Gilgamesh's responses of 4,500 years ago are not all that unfamiliar to us today. First, he tries asceticism. He goes off to the desert alone, gets away from everything and everyone, and simplifies his life. But he discovers this is no way for a human being to live. He concludes that living this way is not what it means to be truly human.

Second, he tries hedonism—wine, women, and song. The barmaid takes him on a journey to the wild side of life. Seize the day, do everything pleasurable; perhaps that is the essence of humanity. But Gilgamesh finds he is still empty.

Third, he sets out to discover the secret of immortality. If he can just live forever, then he'll comprehend the human condition. Gilgamesh knows of one couple who is immortal, namely the Noah and his wife characters in the Sumerian's flood story. It turns out they cannot share the secret of immortality with Gilgamesh; it was just granted to them by God.

Feeling despondent, dejected, depressed, and disheveled, Gilgamesh sets off toward his old city, Uruk. He can think of nothing else to do but to go home. As he approaches the city, he breaks at nightfall to rest. In his tired, dejected state he sets up camp about twenty leagues from the city. In the morning, as the sun rises, Gilgamesh lifts his tired, lifeless eyes and sees the walls of Uruk, his city—the walls he built.

Suddenly he comes fully awake with a start! That is it! He gets it! Human life is with people. We are mortals. We will die. The appropriate response is not asceticism, nor hedonism, nor some vain search for immortality. Instead, it is to live in relationship with other fellow human beings and work for their betterment and the betterment of the world in the time allotted us.

Gilgamesh truly "awoke" at that moment. He became a mature adult. He learned to accommodate himself to mortality. His answer is perhaps the bravest, most steadfast, intellectually honest answer one can attain. Gilgamesh came to understand that the hope of immortality is a sweet, comforting way to look at life. But he concluded it was simply not true. His was not some dreary pessimistic conclusion. The fact is, we are all going to die. Now make good on the time you are given. Be socially responsible, be with and do for others.

Most of us who've grown up in the Christian tradition have not been encouraged to put much stock in hedonism.

And except for monastic orders and a few other eccentric people, we've not been encouraged to seek our answers in asceticism. But we have unquestionably cast our lot firmly in the "search for immortality" response. Traditional Christians do this today by believing in an omnipotent, benevolent God who through his Son gives us immortality and therefore meaning and purpose for our existence. In essence, we become God-like with life eternal.

Do we ever stop to think profoundly about these things? Have we considered our personal answer apart from the cultural answer we've been given? Are we aware of how others, over eons of human experience, have answered this question?

Let's consider the Jewish response, that faith tradition from which Christianity was birthed. Abraham and Moses and Judaic tradition did not think it was appropriate to try to become God-like, nor even to worry too much about the afterlife. Doing so was and is a grave sin. Rather, the Jewish tradition has said the answer lies in being part of God's community on earth. That is how you find your way through this immortality dilemma. Just don't worry too much about it; the most important thing is to be part of God's people here on earth doing God's work. I find it fascinating to attend Jewish funerals and see how differently they deal with the afterlife and immortality issue. Their tradition has much in common with Gilgamesh's answer.

Again, majority Christian tradition says the appearance of mortality is simply not true. The authentic reality, according to Christian tradition, is that you can be immortal, and that you will find it in Jesus Christ. We are only pilgrims here on this mortal earth. We have another home and in that other home, we are immortal. Critics might say this is an escapist's answer, "If you don't like the reality you see, simply say it isn't so and find another reality." Still it works for most Christians.

Does your human experience validate the majority Christian response? Is this a better or more intellectually honest or braver answer than Gilgamesh's, some 4,500 years ago? Would we not do just as well to consider Gilgamesh's answer as equally valid?

Now, at this point, you may think I am anti-Christian or a heretic of the first order. I don't consider myself such! But it is true that I don't necessarily accept the majority viewpoint of what being a Christian today means either. Let me explain with a bit of a historical context.

What attracted outsiders to Christianity in its early years—and still attracts me and others today—is being part of a gathering, joined by a spiritual power, into an extended family.

Consider Christianity's beginnings. I am indebted to Elaine Pagels and her books *The Gnostic Gospels* and *Beyond Belief: The Secret Gospel of Thomas*, from which much of the following information comes. In Rome when the sick visited the temples of the Greek God of healing, they had to pay an enormous sum for healing. When they consulted priests, there was a high price to be paid for herbs and medicine. Christians, in contrast, took no money. Alexandria, Antioch, Carthage, and Rome itself at the time were crowded with people from throughout the known world. Times were tough. The economy was in shambles. Vast shantytowns surrounded the cities where begging, prostitution, and stealing were the norm. Clubs or societies formed for security. Archeological digs have found entry gates and signs from these gathering places. It was almost impossible to live without being part of some club or society.

Most clubs or gatherings were totally self-protective. Christian gatherings, or clubs, were different. Members gave voluntarily to support orphans. They bought food and medicines to the prisoners working in mines. Some Christians bought coffins and dug graves to bury the poor and criminals. Tertullian, an early Christian author, said, "There is no buying and selling of any kind in what belongs to God. There is no compulsion; everything is voluntary."

The usual expectation of the day was that one only took care of one's family. No wonder crowds of people were attracted to Christian groups. Galen, a prominent Greek physician and philosopher, said, "In matters of food and drink, and in keen pursuit of justice, they have attained a level not inferior to that of genuine philosophers."

Christianity created a radically new social structure, and it was good. I applaud that accomplishment. I take personal pride in being part of that Christian tradition.

The Judeo-Christian tradition was also the prime mover, I believe, in the movement toward individual worth and dignity. Joseph Campbell, the great writer about myth, speaks of this attribute of Christianity. Just as I take pride in Christianity's new social structure, I also take pride in being part of this tradition of individual worth and dignity, especially after living in Japan for a time. Individual worth and dignity are not part of Japanese heritage in the same way. From my experience in Japan, I came to understand how much I value this western, and predominantly Judeo-Christian, concept.

I find considerable empathy and connectedness with what Christianity has been at times in its long heritage. A good example is my acquaintance with Meister Eckhart. This late thirteenth–and early fourteenth-century mystic's words still enchant me. "All those who want to make statements about God are wrong, for they fail to say anything about him. Those who want to say nothing about him are right, for no word can express God." Or another well-known quote, "Man's best chance of finding God is to look in the place where he left him." Meister Eckhart's less than orthodox writings were so popular that church authorities brought him to ecclesiastical trial and excommunicated him posthumously. The quotes above come from David Steindl-Rast's book *Meister Eckhart, From Whom God Hid Nothing*. It is what became majority Christian thought and doctrine that I do not relate too, and I doubt if Christianity in its current majority essence will be a viable religion in 500 years unless it changes significantly.

So my plea is not to discard Christianity, but rather to transform it so it can provide value and meaning for the Human Condition for the next 500 years. For me to suggest that we may need to tinker with the stream if the stream is to bring life and hope and meaning for the future is not heresy, but inevitability. We do well to tinker, or the stream may dry up and refresh no one.

I began this paper with the epic of Gilgamesh and his answer to the human condition, "Yes, we are mortal, we each will die." The correct response to that is to live with and to do good for our fellow men and the world around us in the time given us. We suggested that Gilgamesh's answer is not all that far from what some Christians have concluded at times in the past, and certainly not out of the bounds of what a "Christian" response could be going forward. I find it interesting that Jesus is credited with a very similar insight. To paraphrase, he who will save his life will lose it; he that will lose his life for others will save it. At a minimum, we should do no harm!

14

If I Were a Tinker

I MENTIONED IN THE Thinkers Group missive above that my plea is not to discard Christianity, but to transform it into a religion that can be viable for the next 500 years. I also suggested "tinkering" would be necessary for that to happen. Just what tinkering would I suggest?

First, I would encourage all Christians to understand better their own history and tradition. We've come to think our brand of Christianity as evidenced in our place and time is "forever" Christianity. For most early Christians, the focus was on being seekers on a journey, not codifiers or guardians of correct belief. That came later—on into the third and fourth centuries, as Christianity became less of a "club" that facilitated life and cared for its members and became more of an institution supporting the state and other vested interests.

Someone may ask, "How do we transition values and ethics and tradition over the generations without institutions to carry it forward?" Granted, institutions are essential. Think of an institution as the bucket, and values and ethics and tradition as the water. As long as the bucket is kept in good repair, and as long as the water is fresh and life supporting, all is well. We do need institutions to carry our culture forward. But a bucket that no longer holds water, or that fouls its contents, is a useless thing indeed. If we knew more, we might not be shocked when someone says that Christianity could probably be a more viable religion for the future if it would give up some of its human constructs like the Trinity, the incarnation, and the virgin birth.

The Trinity is not even mentioned in the Bible, but it is a doctrine adopted in the fourth century as the church and state collaborated on reaching single-mindedness of doctrine—for political reasons. Karen Armstrong's *The History of God* provides an entertaining account of how a minority human viewpoint among delegates to the Council of Nicaea in AD 325 prevailed, over a position held by the majority. Christians, without any awareness of the other options, have built many a theological fortress on that minority concept in the years since.

And thinking of the incarnation as the indwelling of God in all people as opposed to God dwelling in one "God-man" is not a totally new, or heretical, concept in some Christian circles. The debate at the Council of Chalcedon in AD 451 on this issue makes clear there have always been other ways of thinking about it. Here is a thought-provoking anecdote about incarnation from my own experience: When my daughter was thirteen years old she asked me, "Do you really believe Jesus was the son of God?" to which I replied, "Yes, of course. But then so are you and so am I." She smiled and walked away.

The doctrine of the virgin birth in Christian tradition, as many scholars now tell us, came to us largely because of a mistranslation of a word in the book of Isaiah. According to scholars, the Hebrew word in Isaiah is "almah" meaning young woman. That got translated into the Greek word "Parthenos" meaning sexually pure woman—and the Gospel writers picked up on the Greek word's meaning. Had the Hebrew writer in Isaiah meant "virgin" he would have used the word "bethulah." Also, we know from Joseph Campbell's *An Open Life* that the virgin birth story occurs in many cultures, even in American Indian mythology. Are we ready to believe all of these others as equally and truly historical, which negates the specialness of Jesus' virgin birth, or are we so arrogant as to call all the others a lie? Why not accept it for what it is—a mythic image, in all cultures, of the birth of spiritual life in us as humans? This is just one of those marks that set us apart from the animals.

Second, I think we gain nothing, regarding Christianity's future viability, by reading the Bible literally. The Bible was never intended to be read as a history or science textbook. For many Christians, the Bible becomes nothing short of an idol. We need to understand the Bible in the grand traditions of religious myth, as metaphor; to trust our own understanding and experience as the equal of any existing creed or dogma. For example, as Campbell reminds us in *An Open Life*, there are "saviors" in many traditions, along with their virgin birth and death and resurrection stories. If you have not done so, read about the Jain saviors, the Buddhist saviors, the Hindu saviors, and the saviors in Greek mystery religions. Time and again the savior's death and resurrection becomes a model for the casting off of the old Adam and the unfolding of the new. Unfortunately, in majority Christian tradition, the freeing grace of new birth has become possible only through the doctrines and sacraments of the church. According to the church, we are born into original sin, and the only way out is through the sacraments of the church. That is a narrow gate that makes sense to fewer and fewer people. Instead, let's celebrate that in Christian tradition, as well as in many other traditions, there is the real possibility of one's life moving in one direction, and when that direction proves non-productive, one can "repent" and go in another direction.

Third, we would do well to read and interpret differently those passages some have used for centuries to support Christian exclusivity. It is simply not helpful in a shrinking world to have any religion and its followers absolutely convinced that their religion is the only true religion, not only for themselves but for all others. "I am the way the truth and the life; no man comes to the Father but by me" may make for interesting reading, but why should we interpret that so literally when we don't feel compelled to do the same with, "Greet one another with a holy kiss," or, "He that is wounded in the stones, or hath his privy member cut off, shall not enter in the congregation of the Lord." These are all direct quotes from the Bible, yet we raise one as an absolute religious imperative while ignoring the others.

Fourth, I am convinced that any religion which does not make sacred this earth—our true source of life, along with the sun—will not provide humankind what is needed in the way of life-sustaining religious and spiritual activities. The phrase about being fruitful and multiplying and about having dominion over the earth must give way to the reality of an earth that is over populated relative to the resources it can sustainably provide, and which has not been well cared for by our dominion over it. Fortunately, many Christians are coming to see the light on this issue, an example being the book *Redeeming Creation: The Biblical Basis for Environmental Stewardship* by Van Dyke, Mahan, Sheldon, and Brand. The Bible has many helpful words to say about care of this magnificent creation. We'd do well, in the Christian tradition, to focus more on these words if we hope to see the Christian way viable in 500 years.

Fifth, we would do well to understand the Christian tradition in the context of thousands of years of human existence and religious developments over all those years instead of just since the birth of Jesus. Judeo/Christianity was just one of several truly "world" religions that developed shortly before or after his birth. But we can document thousands of years of human religious experience before that. What was going on then? What gems of religious understanding are we totally ignorant of from those times? Understanding the whole of human religious experience just may provide us the insights we need to create a Christian-like religious framework that will nurture our own spirituality in these and coming postmodern times. As someone said, a religion that cannot survive in the face of knowledge is pure superstition. No doubt the speaker's reference was to the knowledge of science, but consider an example relating to knowledge from the field of religion itself. One of those mainstays of traditional Christianity is that God is the same yesterday, today, and tomorrow. That is simply not true, as evidenced by reviewing Christian writings since Jesus' time. Books such as *The Disappearance of God* by Richard Friedman, *The Origin of Sin* by Elaine Pagels, *Naming the Antichrist* by Robert

Fuller, and *A History of Sin* by Oliver Thomson make clear that not only has God changed, but our concepts of what is good and evil have also changed.

A "Christian" response of this nature may even move Christianity toward viability as a meaningful religion for the coming millennium. We should not be shy about transitioning Christianity in this direction. Others in the past have so transitioned Christianity in keeping with their experience and knowledge of the world around them. After all, the true essence of responding appropriately to the mortality dilemma is caring for one another and for this earth in the time allotted us. That is not an un-Christian message, at least in certain times and places in its long history, and it is certainly a Christian message that would serve us well going forward.

15

Who Am I Today?

If I were selecting from among religions on a shelf today, I would be hard pressed to choose; I could not do so without reference to my past. My life experience is profoundly steeped in the Anabaptist/Mennonite strain of Christian tradition. One can change, of course, but I have found the words of friend and mentor Paul Peachey very enlightening. Paul had many accomplishments, one of which was serving on the faculty at Georgetown University in Washington, DC. Throughout his life, sometimes pushing at the edge of Mennonite thought and practice, Paul always stayed connected to the Mennonite Church. When I asked him why, his response, as paraphrased, was, everybody carries religious baggage—we can switch out that baggage, but why get rid of what I have just to take on someone else's? He continued, "I decided it was better to keep the baggage I was given and to work with it rather than to spend time and energy in search of another—which may also not satisfy for long. I'd rather do what I can to transform the Mennonite faith than to abandon it."

Clearly I did not stringently follow Paul's counsel, but it has aided me in not feeling any need to destroy or malign the bridges I've passed over. Culturally, I still feel very Mennonite. And I have remained a member of the First Mennonite Church in Iowa City,

Iowa, to this day. As regards broader Christendom, I still value Jesus as a principal model for life. That doesn't mean, for me, that other religious figures and traditions are of no value or relegated to the dustbin of idolatry. I have come to treasure the insights or truths revealed in many of the world's spiritual myths and religions. To those who suggest I have no basis for claiming any relationship to Christianity, I remind them that the only thing Christians have agreed upon in the last 2000 years is not to take Jesus or his words very seriously, and certainly not literally, regarding how to live. There have always been great differences in how people experience and live their Christianity. While I fail daily, I do aspire to a Sermon on the Mount ethic, and I take pride in being part of that long-ago tradition of Christians gathering to take care of each other and those around them.

When Dad died in 1997, something truly amazing burst forth. All of Dad's nine children started communicating with each other, via letters, about the deeper things of life. We came to know each other as adults for the first time. Several years after the letters began, one brother calculated that the printing of each letter on a single sheet of paper, and many were longer, would have created a stack of paper five feet tall. It was as if the proverbial cork was pulled from the wine bottle. We started drinking of each other's essence. Was it just coincidence this began immediately after Dad's death? I think not. His over emphasis on one way to live and to think put a damper on any free conversation among his children. Even though my Damascus Road experience finally freed me from my past, it was Dad's death that liberated us siblings to share openly with each other as to who and what we had become as adults. I am often amazed that nine children could come from the same parents and grow up in the same household, but represent such a diaspora as adults. Someday those letters may tell a broader story of my family; for now, they remain private.

While reviewing sibling letters for this book, I discovered a one-page missive I had prepared in October of 1996, in response to a challenge. Someone challenged me to talk about the transcendence of God in three minutes or less. My response to that challenge is the following:

Three minutes to discuss the transcendence of God is not much time when some of the world's greatest thinkers have spent a lifetime doing so; still I will try. Someone made the comment, "He who gazes at the stars unavoidably starts thinking." My first morning chore, as the youngest boy growing up on the farm, was to go out in the pitch dark of early morning and bring in the cows from the pasture for milking. I came to know the sky and the constellations almost as well as the hay loft. One can't help but think about the universe when gazing at the stars, especially if you combine observation with some reading about the incredible universe in which we live and move and have our being. In comparing ourselves to what seems to be the infinite expanse above, we realize we are a mere speck of dust. And then we go to school and find out there is another apparent infinity—that which is infinitely small—the atom, and now even smaller particles.

When thinking of the cosmos or the microscopic, it is easy for me to give God back his essential quality, which is to exist beyond anything we can conceive. If God exists, then he must be where human knowledge cannot reach him. Otherwise, he or she is not God, and all our characterizations of God are but idolatry.

But it is at this intersection of the cosmos and the microscopic that we must live. Strictly speaking, traditional Christianity represents a form of idolatry. It is not God one believes in, but an image of God—and if it is not an image made of wood or stone, it is certainly a portrait constructed of words. Think of all the personal words we have for God. At least, in Old Testament times they solved the problem of naming God in a divine manner, "I am that I am." We, on the other hand, have no fear of making God only an extension of ourselves writ large, for example, "Our Father." With these thoughts it is easy to understand Pascal's comment, "To believe in God means to doubt God," or from St. Augustine who said, "If you understand God, it is not God you understand." Einstein is credited with saying, "A personal God is a relic from medieval times surviving only in the minds where either medieval darkness or the happy simplicity of the naïf hold sway." Whatever we think of Einstein's comment, there is another point of reference other than the cosmos and microscopic, and that is this earth—the soil, the air, the structures in which we live. Here, our relatively small, and sometimes unpleasant, lives are played out. We do this and we do that, go about our work, struggle with crises big and small, amuse ourselves, fulfill our desires and find new dreams, make decisions, meet people and forget people.

Compared to the cosmos and the microscopic, this life here in our world is so insignificant—and yet for each and every one of us, it represents the real world, our only world. My personal universe is the life I lead, not the Big Bang Theory, nor the quirks of Chaos Theory. So, how to find meaning in this life we live? There is something to be said for death as the focus of meaning in our lives, but three minutes does not provide time to analyze that one. Maybe for these three minutes, and for this life we lead, as someone has suggested, these three overused, worn out words are the best we can do—namely faith, humor, and love. I might substitute "awe and wonder" for faith, but faith (or awe and wonder) alone leads to bigotry and arrogance; humor alone leads to cynicism; and love alone leads to obsession. Together they are not just the best we can do; they make for a great existence. And we can still sweeten that existence by pondering the infinite above and all around us.

I would be remiss in closing if I did not join in the humility expressed by an old Jewish proverb, "Man thinks and God laughs!"

Reviewing all those sibling letters also reminded me of how much traditional Christianity puts a focus on belief. As I have expressed, a religious focus on correct belief or adherence to specific dogma or doctrine has not worked for me in years. Having said that, the results of a survey based on belief provided me with an interesting outcome. The organization Beliefnet distributed an exercise entitled *Belief-O-Matic* on its Web site in 2001. In response to a long sequence of questions, *Belief-O-Matic* provided respondents with their level of compatibility with the world's religions. *Belief-O-Matic* informed me I was 100 percent compatible with Liberal Quakers and 99 percent compatible with Unitarian Universalists. I was least compatible with Conservative Christian/ Protestant groups.

Correct belief is so embedded in Christian thought it is no surprise that in our sibling letters, challenges were made to state what one believes. In a letter written in February of 2000, I responded as follows.

1. I believe that science provides the best explanation for the existence of our universe, referred to as the Big Bang. I don't know, and it doesn't matter to me if the Big Bang was a "creating" event or simply a "transitional" happening of some prior energy/force/matter into some new form. I like the concept that in the Big Bang some inconceivably powerful energy/ force shared its very essence with everything that is the universe now. We are part of that essence, as are the trees, the wind, the oceans, and birds. While some of that energy/force is in us, it is not limited to us; it transcends the physical aspect of the universe—and I am comfortable calling that God.

2. I believe our task in this life is to become a truly "individuated self" to use Jung's language, to "be all we can be" to use the Army's slogan; to do this not by escaping this world, but by finding our place in this world. I believe when we allow the great possibilities of life to enter into us, and when we embrace them, then we are most individual—and most connected to the whole. It is a journey into wholeness.

3. I believe our soul is best cared for, not by solving all the puzzles and mysteries of life (though that is a great and honorable endeavor), but by an appreciation of the paradoxical mysteries that blend light and darkness into the grandeur of what human life and culture can be. To cite one example, the paradox that one truly finds one's life by losing it, is a grand

mystery, and most sacred traditions have found it so. I believe the language of the soul is myth, ritual, and poetry.

4. I believe that to be in good health or to be whole, everyone needs to come to some world view, a scheme of values and a sense of relatedness to the whole. I believe there are multiple frameworks within which one can do this. Traditional or classical Christianity is just one example; it is not the one for me.

5. I believe the Bible is at its best when it is looked to for insight, when it is a stimulus for religious imagination, for searching the heart for its deepest and most exalted possibilities. The Bible is at its worst when it is approached as a history or scientific text; or for moral certainty, for miraculous proofs of faith; or for the avoidance of doubt or process in making life's difficult choices.

6. I believe that a good balance for what some point out as the possible excesses of existentialism and nihilism is, to use concepts from Jung, "the God within in moral discourse with others." Through reflection, a person can find their cosmic moorings by cultivating and coming to know the God within, along with serious conversation about things moral with others. We do need to be in relationship with others to find our own way. For me, this approach presents no inherent conflict between spirituality and science, nor any inherent presumptions about one religious experience being superior to others.

7. I believe that in the care of one's soul, insight is more useful than truth. Truth is a stopping point asking for commitment and defense. Insight is a starting point on the journey to wholeness.

8. I believe the poem, "The Journey," by Mary Oliver, expresses my experience so well. After recounting in poetic form all the outside voices that hammer at us, she concludes the poem with the thought that the only life any of us can save is our own.

16

A Book Ending for a Life Ongoing

SOMEONE ONCE ASKED ME how I could read Habakkuk 3:17–19 and not be convinced of a personal God. The passage from the New International Version reads, "Though the fig tree does not bud and there are no grapes on the vines, though the olive crop fails and the fields produce no food, though there are no sheep in the pen and no cattle in the stalls, yet I will rejoice in the Lord, I will be joyful in God my Savior. The Sovereign Lord is my strength; He makes my feet like the feet of a deer; He enables me to tread on the heights." I responded with my paraphrase of the passage as I interpreted its meaning for me, as follows: "Life is difficult; it is mortal! But that is OK because in the living of this life I have been on a journey discovering the essence of being and wholeness, and in finding my place in the greater universe. In so doing, I have found joy and strength and insights I never imagined!"

Those words attributed to Jesus in Luke 11:9, New International Version—"So I say to you, ask and it will be given to you; search, and you will find; knock, and the door will be opened to you"—have been both an inspiration for, and an affirmation of, my odyssey from Mennonite boy to a man of considerable years. My Damascus Road experience was a high point on the journey.

It solidified a direction I'd been on for almost two decades and affirmed an on-going process of seeking and finding.

I find it interesting there seems to be a consensus among scholars that Buddhism as a religion has fewer inherent contradictions vis-à-vis science than any other of the world's religions. In recognition of that, I close with a story from Buddhist folklore. The story is that a traveling Brahmin, a Hindu priest, came upon the Buddha meditating under a tree. The Brahmin began questioning the Buddha, "Who are you?" After multiple inquiries, the Buddha finally responded, "I am one who awoke."

May the same be said of me—and of each of you.

Bibliography

Armstrong, Karen. *A History of God: The 4000-Year Quest of Judaism, Christianity and Islam*. New York: Alfred A. Knoff, 1993.

Auel, Jean. *Clan of the Cave Bear: Earth's Children*. New York: Bantam, 2002.

Barks, Coleman, Trans. *The Essential Rumi*. Edison, NJ: Harper Castle Books, 1991.

Berry, Ruth. *Jung: A Beginner's Guide*. London: Hodden and Stoughton, 2000.

Bly, Robert. *Iron John*. Reading, MA: Addison-Wesley, 1990.

Borg, Marcus. *Jesus: A New Vision*. Harper San Francisco, 1987.

———. *Meeting Jesus Again for the First Time: The Historical Jesus and the Heart of Contemporary Faith*. Harper San Francisco, 1995.

Campbell, Joseph. *The Flight of the Wild Gander*. New York: Harper Perennial, 1990.

———. *The Hero with a Thousand Faces*. Princeton, NJ: Bollinger Series XVII, Princeton University Press, 1968.

Campbell, Joseph, and Toms, Michael. *An Open Life: Joseph Campbell in Conversation with Michael Toms*. New York: Harper Perennial, 1990.

Davies, Paul. *God and the New Physics*. New York: Simon & Schuster, 1983.

Darwin, Charles. *The Descent of Man*. London: Penguin Classics, 2004.

Friedman, Richard. *The Disappearance of God: A Divine Mystery*. Boston: Little, Brown and Company, 1995.

Fuller, Robert. *Naming the Antichrist*. Oxford University Press, USA, 1996.

Funk, Robert. *Honest to Jesus: Jesus for a New Millennium*. Harper San Francisco, 1996.

Greenleaf, Robert K. *The Servant Leader*. Indianapolis, IN: The Robert K. Greenleaf Center, 1991, originally 1970.

Harder, Leland, and Kauffman, J. Howard. *Anabaptists Four Centuries Later*. Scottsdale, PA: Herald, 1975.

Johnson, Robert A. *He*. New York: Harper Perennial, 1989.

———. *Owning Your Own Shadow: Understanding the Dark Side of the Psyche*. Harper San Francisco, 1991.

———. *She,* Revised Edition. New York: Harper Perennial, 1989.

Mack, Burton. *Who Wrote the New Testament: The Making of Christian Myth*. Harper San Francisco, 1995.

McCauley, Deborah Vansau. *Appalachian Mountain Religion: A History*. Urbana: University of Illinois Press, 1995.

Meier, Carl Alfred, MD. *Jung's Analytical Psychology and Religion*. Carbondale: Southern Illinois University Press, Feffer and Simons, Inc., Arcturus Books Edition, 1977.

Meyer, William. *Darwin in a New Key: Evolution and the Question of Value*. Eugene: Cascade Books, an imprint of Wipf and Stock, 2016.

Mlodinow, Leonard. *The Upright Thinkers: The Human Journey from Living in Trees to Understanding the Cosmos*. New York: Pantheon Books, 2015.

Morgan, Elaine. *The Aquatic Ape: A Theory of Human Evolution*. New York: Stein and Day, 1982.

Mortimer, John. *The First and Second Rumpole Omnibus*. London: Penguin Books, 1983 and 1988.

O'Neal, David, Ed., Steindl-Rast, David, Foreword. *Meister Eckhart, From Whom God Hid Nothing*. Boston: Shambhala, 1996.

Pagels, Elaine. *Beyond Belief: The Secret Gospel of Thomas*. New York: Vintage Books/Random House, 2003.

————. *The Gnostic Gospels*. New York: Vintage Books/Random House, 1979.

————. *The Origin of Sin*. New York: Random House, 1995.

Peck, Scott. *The Road Less Traveled: A New Psychology of Love, Traditional Values and Spiritual Growth*. New York: Simon & Schuster, 1978.

Rees, Martin J. *Our Cosmic Habitat*. Princeton: Princeton University Press, 2001.

Ruhl, Jerry. *Robert A. Johnson: Balancing Heaven and Earth*. New York: Harper One, 1998.

Spong, John Shelby. *A New Christianity for a New World*. Harper San Francisco, 2001.

Staguhn, Gerhard. *God's Laugher: Physics, Religion and the Cosmos*. New York: Kodansha International, 1994.

Swimme, Brian, and Berry, Thomas. *The Universe Story: A Celebration of the Unfolding of the Cosmos*. Harper San Francisco, 1994.

Thomson, Oliver. *A History of Sin*. New York: Barnes and Noble Books, 1993.

Van Dyke, Mahan, Sheldon and Brand. *Redeeming Creation: The Biblical Basis for Environmental Stewardship*. Downers Grove, IL: InterVarsity Press, 1996.

Wade, Nicholas. *Before the Dawn: Recovering the Lost History of Our Ancestors*. New York: Penguin, 2007.